Finding God
in the Rubble of Numbers

Finding God
in the Rubble of Numbers

Ruth M. Penksa, gnsh

authorHOUSE®

AuthorHouse™
1663 Liberty Drive
Bloomington, IN 47403
www.authorhouse.com
Phone: 1-800-839-8640

Published by AuthorHouse   02/26/2013

ISBN: 978-1-4817-1551-5 (sc)
ISBN: 978-1-4817-1550-8 (e)

Library of Congress Control Number: 2013902635

One

Dedication: "I Owe You"

I owe you, God. . . .

I believe that God has encouraged me to write this book. How do I know? I know because of the ways he slipped brief distractions into my ordinary prayer suggesting ideas. It's because I had committed to including God's word in a reflection after each memoir. I know because as I begin to write, I am praying for an inspiration for a reflection. The answer comes as a thought or when I flip the bible open and receive an aha!

Thank you God for providential "distractions" and "directions" you offer me.

I owe you, all the characters in my stories . . .

Whether you are living or deceased you have been at the heart of my memories. Some of you are named, others remain nameless. Others of you have been identified with new names that still allow the story to unfold.

Thank you for being a part of my life experiences.

I owe you, all who have reminded me of events to share . . .

How often have I sat with you and engaged in everyday chatter only to find a memory emerging. Sometimes you have filled in the holes of my memory or corrected my version of a story. Or you have been the memory itself.

Thank you for the scoops and storytelling that brought back memories.

I owe you, all who took time to read "The Scoop on Ruth" . . .

I appreciate your taking the time and interest to plow through my first effort. It was good to hear your comments about the parables—my stories—and the reflections. I was encouraged by so many who found themselves or their own stories somewhere in my pages, for allowing my memoirs to resound in your life and prayer.

Thank you for "your read" that inspired me to continue with another Scoop . . . on "Finding God in the Rubble of Numbers"

I owe you, for your special gift or contribution toward this publication . . .

What makes a book finally happen? What we see: a providential meeting with a gifted Jeff Feinman resulted in his creating this exciting book cover. What we don't see: Self publishing requires financial support. Behind the scenes is my religious congregation's generous contribution toward publication.

Thank you for your gifts that are realized in every "Finding God" . . . that finds itself on a book shelf.

Two

About the Author—unknown me

My numbers break open the story of my life experiences. They are the revelation of who I am, this person who is the author of a second book.

I enjoy being called an author. As such, I have chosen a style to tell each numbered—story followed by a scriptural reflection to carry on the theme.

I am a Buffalo gal, born and reared in the Black Rock and Riverside areas—14207—of the City. My family nurtured me in the tradition of our Polish heritage and Catholic faith.

While schooling was important my parents themselves had limited educations. My dad was a blue collar worker in defense plants. My mom worked in a variety of factory positions. Both had avocations as musicians. Dad played the saxophone, guitar and other instruments. He and his brothers were members of a family band. Mom was a snare drummer in a marching unit and a great harmonica player. They often joined musical relatives for Saturday night "hoe downs" in our home. Unfortunately, this not-so-musical daughter was relegated to listening.

My forte in my growing up years was art. It dominated my free time, my high school studies and my aspirations to pursue a career in art. The years before college found me involved in Church and volunteer activities. They found me working in a deli and at Woolworths. My interests were playing and coaching basketball, softball and ping pong and directing one act plays. I dabbled in skiing but fell out of love of the sport. In the early history of TV, reading remained my entry into other worlds and ideas.

By the time I was in college art was becoming a weak avocation. Teaching was my interest and I graduated with Spanish major. Later I would pursue post graduate studies in Spanish, theology and philosophy.

During my d'Youville College days the librarian, a Grey Nun, had suggested that teaching was an avocation, that I should find my life "vocation". That nudged me and a developing thought about becoming a nun. The day came with a decision. I would become a nun—a Grey Nun of the Sacred Heart. Now my life would be dotted with a new variety of experiences—in education, in teaching, administration and in a variety of ministries . . .

When I retired from Erie Community College-City in 2007, I had been a Campus Minister and adjunct professor of Spanish for 25 years.

It was shortly before retiring that I began to write my first book, *The Scoop on Ruth*. The book left much unsaid, unwritten and begged for more pages. Thus the author, Ruth, adventured into another book and the place where readers may check "my numbers" to learn more about this unknown author—Me.!

Three

Preface: In the Beginning—

. . . there was a formless void and God said "let there be".

Then there was my dad whose dear friend had called him "the funniest man I know". And there were teachers too, whose gifts introduced me to language and how to use it to experience my growing world.

<u>My Dad</u>. Yes, he was a funny man. He enjoyed jokes—mostly puns and slightly, only slightly, off color humor.

What I remember most was how he shared the funnies with me. I was around six years old and an only child. Sunday mornings I would hop into his bed and he would read the comics and often with his vocal characterization of the people. Then there was the radio. I grew up pre-TV. My dad would tune in to a radio program where Mayor Fiorello La Guardia of New York City read the newspaper comics during a newspaper strike. We would stretch out on the floor and my dad urged me to follow along as the Mayor read in his high, squeaky voice.

<u>My Teachers</u>. As a Spanish teacher, I am always baffled about how I learned to speak and write good English. The reason, Spanish grammar behaves; it keeps close to its rules. Not so English. English will tease one when presented with its exceptions—words like foot or boot. Is there a rule that distinguishes the sounds of "oo"? English emerged as my language from years of those teachers' artful gifs of opening its world of possibility to unsuspecting students.

I remember tiles on our classroom desk and forming words, copying them from the blackboard. I remember Dick and Jane. But what took me way beyond those? As I passed from grade to grade I was experiencing a gradual development of skills. My teachers recognized my writing ability and encouraged my writing compositions for certain occasions.

I was fortunate to grow up with those influences. It was my dad and his reading of the Sunday comics from the News that opened the way. The other was having many good teachers to develop my skills and interest in reading and writing and the awareness of people and things. Together, these dad and teacher influences brought me to enjoy reading and writing and to encourage visits to the library early in my life. That library that welcomed my frequent visits, no longer stands at Grant and Amherst Streets. Its final place remains in my memory.

It was a beginning. As I look back I claim all as "good".

Only very late in my life did I even think of writing a book. What would I write about? The answer appeared in the words of someone who claimed:" write about what you know best—yourself." A good idea! Yet, I was stalemated when I considered an autobiography. First, how to do it! Second, who'd care about me? The possibility came not as an autobiography but memoirs accompanied by scriptural reflections. In that case the reader is drawn from my story into his own. Thus, The Scoop on Ruth was born and the reader would get glimmers of my story in random order.

Now, I invite the reader to consider my second book. I continue the tales of my life and scriptural reflection style (what I referred to as "parables"). Again, I present my story in random order. This time I searched for episodes related to numbers—addresses, years, comments, prices, dates, ages, room numbers . . . whatever, reminders of events in my life to lead you along in no particular life order except to follow the numbers.

. . . on the 7th day he rested from all the work he had done.

Now, in the pages that follow I offer another Scoop: on "<u>Finding God in the Rubble of Numbers</u>". Once more I invite you to into the rubbles of my life, this time via the numbers that triggered so many memories.

Now, I invite you to read about the book and why numbers. Then open the book to the sections and my numbers and begin the journey through the rubble with me . . .

Four

About the Book—Why Numbers?

As I thought of writing a second book my mind drifted toward a theme to draw out my thoughts. I don't know when numbers** became the tool, the angle I'd use to tell my stories. Perhaps it was my frequent trips down Hertel Avenue that suggested the use of numbers. I would glance to the left at a small shop and memories of my dad and his watch repair shop would quickly emerge. Vivid pictures flashed in my mind's eye—dad bent over his work bench or standing in front of the shop near a window marked "Jewelry Repair". Today my eye rests on the number—638 . . . the same number, the address of the shop of my memories.

The first episode I wrote thus emerged—"638 The Watchmaker's Shop". It was a deciding moment. I would reach into my life to tell the stories based on the numbers that would be associated with each. Thus I began to seek out those numbers. They might refer to dates, years, months, addresses, age, room numbers, school numbers, grades in school, a count of items or people . . . . and on and on. The point—each provoked a story to tell.

However, the real story—the story intended for the reader is hidden in the scriptural reflection that follows each episode. Here the reader is exposed to the Word of God. Here the reader will find the place for his story and is able to find God in the rubble of his own life and numbers if he but listen.

, , , , ,

Although each episode is related to a number, they were written randomly. The reader will read them in numerical order beginning with "1" and ending with . . ."?"

Something came to my attention as I was well into writing. I received an email that asked the question: "Do you know why 1 is "one", 2 is "two", 3 is "three", 4 is "four" . . . . I enjoyed the logic that traced them 1-9. that attached number with its numeral. The answer is "There are angles!" Very interesting is: "0"!

For a peek at numbers from this angle, for your information—be it fact or fiction, I have included pictures and internet info showing the primitive forms of numbers known as Arabic algorithms*** rather than roman algorithms. However the queen of internet encyclopedias—Wikipedia debunks the theory as urban myth.

For me, myth or not, as I reflected on my writing, I realized that I had been doing just that—checking out the angles associated with each number that told a story and finding God in the rubble of those numbers.

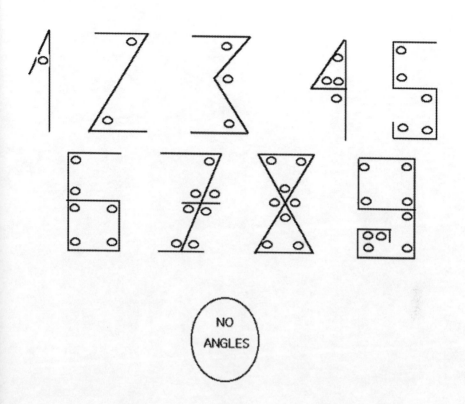

NO ANGLES

11

Family and Folks...

together they enliven one's life.

"like the parts of a watch, all of creation with its parts belongs to a whole"

The Watchmaker's Shop

638

1

Once Upon a Family Time

Is there something your family did . . . just once? That is, once all together, at a particular event? Today reminded me of such a "once" in our family experience. As I prayed this morning on Holy Family Sunday I mused on family members living and deceased and prayed for all our intentions. It was then I recalled a "once all together" experience. A rarity among the entire goings on in the family! It happened in All Saints Church, our parish.

Oh yes, I remember childhood days and family visits. On those Sunday gatherings we were kind of together. But the adults were doing their thing and we kids were off doing ours. There were summer outings or vacations at the beach but my dad wasn't there with us enjoying a swim, tossing horseshoes or toasting marshmallows after dark. I don't think he owned a swim suit, sneakers or jeans.

And the movies? Mom loved them. We sometimes went together—mom, we four kids and even friends who joined us. And there were those kids' Saturday afternoons at the movies—two pictures, cartoons and a sequel or maybe just twenty five cartoons. Rarely together and never my dad! I wonder now if he ever went to the movies at all.

Meals? Mom would be busy serving us and then sit down at the last minute, often taking our leftovers to complete her plate. Dad's slogan was he'd sit down "after the kids eat". Was it because we were a chatty disturbance or because of his personal menu—of his choice of pigs' feet or other strange foods? Yet, he often treated us with his version of vegetable soup—one his sons still

15

make today. His sons. On Sundays mom dressed the boys for a special walk in the park probably to watch a ball game. I would be off to play with friends. For mom it was a quiet time for a working woman's respite.

Holidays would start out as a family thing and then find that adult-child separation at work. My dad usually found his way back to his "bench"—that place where strewn watch parts were in the process of being cleaned or repaired, where his skills at this activity occupied so much of his free time.

Our experience of church was divided as well. Mom and dad attended Vespers at Assumption Parish in Black Rock—prayed in polish on Sunday evenings. Attendance at Mass was determined by our Sunday plans so mom or others of us might go alone or in pairs or with friends. But I never knew dad to go to Mass. One Friday, after an evening out with dad, my mom woke me to share some news. "Your father is going to confession on Saturday and to Mass on Sunday". The news was exciting to my teen ears but I smiled and I turned to fall asleep once more.

Sunday would be the celebration of the feast of the Holy Family in the season of Christmas. How appropriate that dad, like Joseph, would be there—dad . . . head of our family. And, the best part was we were all going to attend Mass together. The picture is as clear as I first remembered. As I recall it, I see us lined up near the altar rail to receive Communion . . . I see us from behind . . . . Mom, Sonny, me, the twins—Tom and Mick—and my dad. We were all together at this very special 'once upon a family time"—on the feast of the Holy Family. Almost as if to recognize the specialty of the occasion, an eight year old Mick turned to my dad and encouraged him: "If you don't know what to do, just watch me."

The Holy Family—Joseph, Mary, Jesus. What were their "all together" family moments? The bible doesn't reveal much about their activities. We can imagine a father teaching his son some things about wood working or maybe a mother helping him to read and write. Daily living in a small town would lend itself to each family member having specific chores or ones done in pairs.

What we do know is that this was a typical Jewish family living in a time when much of family life was indeed a shared experience. The Law was dominant as was the observance of prayer, holy days and traditions. Much required a family effort and participation.

When I think of the Holy Family, I imagine the scenes from stories so familiar to us as Christians. Scenes of their all together experiences! I see the clan of people headed toward Bethlehem for the census and Joseph leading the donkey bearing a pregnant Mary. In Bethlehem I look into the stable and see the babe surrounded by his mom and dad. When it was time for the circumcision and naming of the child I see the three receiving the blessing of Simeon and hearing the prophetess Anna proclaim their son as redeemer. On the flight into Egypt Mary is seated on a colt holding her newborn son and Joseph walking beside them. On the return the young boy walks along with his parents.

There comes a first separation when the family starts out to Jerusalem for the custom of Passover. Jesus is twelve. As many children do at that age, he goes off to do his own thing. Later, another separation—the passing of Joseph makes Mary and Jesus into a new family unit.

But a day would yet come to mark a "once in a family time together" that would be enduring and assuring. The words were spoken from the cross to Mary: "Woman, behold your son."; to his beloved disciple: "Behold, your mother". It is a new Holy Family. It is one that invites us, the disciples of other centuries, to now celebrate our new "family time all together" with Mary our Mother.

3

An Evening at Paula's

It was the eve of Paula's birthday, January 3rd. A motley group of her friends gathered around her table for dinner, chatting and singing "Happy Birthday dear Paula". Paula, the secretary to the President of ECC in 1982 when I came to the college as Campus Minister!

What does such a group talk about? My friendship with Paula has brought me in touch with Louise, Jo Mary and Linda, her dear friends whom I might visit once or twice a year. So, I know little of their lives or interests. But put five women together . . . well talk we did.

The obvious seasonal question and answers were shared. How was your Christmas? How did you spend New Year's Eve? I listened as unfamiliar names and events revealed each one's story.

The stories that had gathered us this particular evening were Paula herself and the Christmas story. We were like Magi coming to proclaim our greetings in this home, Paula's home. Each of us came following our individual stars—our personal stories of friendship with Paula, came bearing gifts. And Paula had prepared the table as she had done at so many gatherings before. A birthday remembrance and a meal! Friends gathered to remember!

I suspect it was more than the Christmas season that turned our conversation to religion. We talked about the Church of today and of the past. Questions were turned toward me—not Ruth or

19

the friend, but the Grey Nun, student of theology and philosophy, eager witness to the faith. In the cultural season of expressing "spirituality" rather than claiming a "religion" I welcomed our conversation about religion and the Catholic faith. Even more, I knew that this time together was now a late Christmas blessing, when Jesus was in our midst where five of us had gathered that evening.

But what of Paula's story and my long friendship with her? The pages of our relationship opened on a college Campus. Paula was a seasoned secretary to the president and I was a new Campus Minister on a new campus—newly located in this, the "Old Post Office" building in Buffalo. What first meeting brought us together is unrecorded in our quarter century of friendship. No question that our common religion and faith were part of that meeting and remain a grounding factor to this day.

Today Paula is a secretary to a president once more. Her move was from an educational to a business setting—Pepsi Cola (Buffalo's favorite). In this business setting, I know that Paula brings a strong witness to her faith commitment. Yet, somehow I see Paula misplaced. Her real gifts are not locked into business matters but expressed in a life devoted to family, friends and her God.

One sees in Paula a mirror of Jesus' life as priest, prophet and king—the roles emanating from her baptism and confirmed life. Her response brings her to an adoration of God at Mass and his invitation to "take and eat", to leave Mass and live the dismissal "go forth to love and serve the Lord and one another". In one way or another, her family, the sick and homebound, Confirmation candidates, church societies and members, her three legged cat companion, and all of us who name her "friend" have received her service offered in love. Paula offers leadership and inspires us to model her as she continues to pursue her religious and spiritual development and growth.

I found myself at a special person's birthday gathering that evening. It was her celebration but she was also the host. She had prepared the meal, sat down at table with some friends and invited us to take and eat . . . and to talk.

I went home, recalled the evening and the cheery host whom I call friend. Then memories flooded my thoughts and gratitude pumped a heartbeat for having met her those many years ago.

———————————

I wonder what the first disciples thought about their meeting with Jesus. It seems that each either experienced an unexpected meeting or was introduced to him. Scripture is somewhat vague about where and when and their identification as fishermen, tax collector, brothers of, sons of . . . It is Jesus who becomes the host. It is he who makes the invitations: "Come and See" . . . "Follow me" . . . "I will make you fishers of men" . . .

When they finally gather to walk with Jesus, don't you wonder what they had to say to each other? Surely they whispered the word Messiah among themselves. However, it would be Jesus himself whose life and actions were opened before them that would stimulate their questions, questions about his way of thinking and acting. They would call him "teacher" but "priest, prophet and king"? Their relationship with Jesus would gradually, and even too late, recognize their host, the one with whom they had spent three years.

Yes, I went home, recalled the evening and I knew with whom it was that I have been walking, a recognition of my host-friend of over twenty five years and that One, who for all of us has called us throughout our life.

5

"Betcha-a-Nickel"

The words were printed on the lid of a small decorated wooden box and given me as a gift. The phrase continued," we'll always be friends".

"Betcha a nickel!" There was nothing significant about that expression except that it belongs to me. Anyone who knows me has heard it, and likely more than once. Anyway that expression has become identified with me. I suspect many people have some expression peculiar to them. Perhaps people tease them, as they do me when I begin "Betcha" and they jump in immediately with "a nicklel".

When and why did that expression become mine? What was the event that first urged the words to be spoken? And, what spurred me on to continue using it and in every possible situation when I suggested that I was right?

The small box, my little treasure has been on my dresser now for three decades and counting. For those many years the message-bearing gift has been a reminder of Mary Ann, my top Spanish student. It was her gift to me when I was leaving OLV High School in Pennsylvania to teach in Buffalo, New York.

We had experienced a teacher-student friendship during those Melrose days (the common name for OLV because of its location). Students who have a favorite teacher often "hang around" after school. Those times become ones of sharing something of themselves—about family, favorite TV shows, life issues . . . a time of laughing, teasing and familiarity. That's how it was with Mary Ann. When she graduated, we stayed in touch and we were experiencing a new relationship. I was invited into her post high school life—college, family, marriage, children, and her graduate doctorate degree.

Mary Ann and I have enjoyed our treasure—our friendship, even at a distance. No surprise then when the invitation arrived. It read:

Please be my guest at my inauguration
as the fourteenth president of the College of Saint Benedict.

My response was immediate. In turn Mary Ann arranged for my hospitality with the Benedictine sisters and the courtesy care of the past president of the college. She had made me a very special guest at the weekend celebration of events. One would have suspected that I was responsible for her honored appointment as president.

What gift would I give to honor Mary Ann and this special time of her life? She already knew of our mutual friendship and that was already a gift from One who "knew that ever and ever since life began, our being friends was His plan".

My chosen gift sits on her desk. It is a pen holder with a nickel on the plate that just reads "Betcha a nickel . . ." and Mary Ann knows we'll always be friends.

———————

"Do not store up for yourselves treasures on earth . . ." we are warned. Yet, Jesus speaks of finding a pearl of great price and buying it. He says that the pearl is like the kingdom of Heaven.

I believe that friendship is such a pearl, a treasure. It is something precious, something to take care of, to preserve, and to enjoy. Like the pearl of great price, friendship radiates the promise of the kingdom. Its value is in the message of joy that one finds in such a treasure.

Isn't that joy our hope, a promise—to finally be experienced in the bosom of God? Friendship is an earthly treasure that will find new life in the kingdom. While we hold it here on earth, we recognize the good pearl. But, rather than store it up, selfishly, we surrender its value to Jesus who has called love of neighbor the great commandment.

I betcha a nickel . . . that Mary Ann and I will always be friends—both here on earth and in the kingdom.

6

Miss Jackson

Do you remember a special teacher in your life? Recently, the name of my 6th grade teacher kept coming to mind as I prayed, in general, for all who have affected my academic growth.

Miss Jackson! The name and memories rose out of an eleven year old's classroom experience into the present recognition of their influence. They are the indelible marks written on the early pages of my life and visible throughout these many years. Yes, visible in whom I am but not always clearly identified.

I vaguely remember the woman herself. But, I think she was tall and straight with dark hair and gently chiseled face. Her manner was kind yet firm. I remember how reading, language, words and pronunciation were all important to Miss Jackson.

I looked forward to our Friday afternoon reading sessions. They began with transforming the front desks in each of the six rows. They were turned to face the class. Then, on consecutive weeks, each student in the row took a turn to be seated there and share a few pages from a favorite library book with our student audience. I looked forward to those readings and especially to be able to present mine. I loved to read and to read aloud, to present my chosen book to my classmates.

Today one of my strong interests is reading. Even alone I find that at times I hear myself as the words slip into an audible whisper. I love to read to others as well. Miss Jackson encouraged us to read and God gifted me with an acceptable reading voice. I share that love at Holy Mass as I stand in front of our congregation to read from a favorite book—the Bible. Fridays find me seated before a microphone, reading from a variety of magazines or books. The readings are taped. My audience is folks who are blind or disabled yet hungry to hear the stories and articles.

At dismissal time, Miss Jackson lined us up, thirty or so students anxious to leave. Often we were held up as she prompted the correct pronunciation of an oft misspoken word. "Go to the back of the line", she'd order, if one mispronounced the word of the day. It might have been "libRary" not "libAry". or, "ValentiNes' day" not "ValentiMes' day", "FebRuary not "FebUary.

Even today, I cringe to hear words mispronounced or misused. I wonder who the teachers for some of our media were as I correct them audibly from the comfort of my recliner.

One significant impression Miss Jackson made on me in a very personal way was an introduction to the word "incongruous". Now, how many people remember a particular word taught you by a teacher let alone sixty plus years ago. Imagine an eleven year old carrying that word into her future! I don't recall if the word appeared in a language or geography class or in our reading sessions. Miss Jackson paused to assist us, offering an example. In her own words she explained that sometimes, even in the poverty of southern Blacks, a family would own a piano. It seemed not to match—an expensive instrument in the midst of poverty—that would be "incongruous". But the piano served to uphold their dignity . . . something all of us deserve.

Without dwelling on that word over the many years of my life, its meaning seems to have emerged in my actions and choices. When she presented the word in context, I vowed that I would someday choose to help the impoverished. Perhaps the word was hidden in my discernment to enter a congregation whose charism speaks of "hands to the needy". When I served as a Campus Minister, often a student would appear in expensive sneakers or jeans yet seeking some monetary help. To the criticizing onlookers who saw the wealth in clothing, I imitated a great teacher and I simply introduced them to a new word—"incongruous".

I suspect that we all have a special teacher, a Miss Jackson, hovering in memory and waiting to be recognized in the "me" of another day.

One great teacher was Jesus.

It's interesting that the boy Jesus was about eleven or twelve years old when he sat among the teachers who asked questions and were astonished that he responded with unusual understanding.

When he emerged to begin his ministry, the adult Jesus went about teaching and even introduced his disciples to "parables". And I think when Jesus went away to pray he was opening his Father's book, absorbing the message. Perhaps it was as though "reading" it, speaking it in an audible whisper, were in preparation for proclaiming it aloud in word and action.

He taught those messages wherever his audience was—on the shores of Galilee, near the mountains, on the plain in front of huge crowds, in the Temple. Matthew, in chapter 5, reveals the many teachings of Jesus. I also imagine him seated among clerics and teachers, they at their desks, scrolls opened to read the Scriptures. Instead, it is Jesus who breaks open the Word and introduces the true meaning to rigid and old ideas. He taught them a new word—"love".

Jesus, our teacher! It behooves us to turn toward him as he speaks and allow the authority of his word to be the indelible mark on us, inspiring us and directing our lives so that we may not be sent to the end of the line.

10

Nehi Orange

First dates are kind of special. Mine was when I was in the 7th grade. My date was named Richard. In those days dates began around seven in the evening. But when did one come home? I sought the answer from my mom. Her reply: "You'll know when." The decision became mine. It was one I did not know how to make. Why did my mom leave it to me? It was always like that. There was no discipline that I ever remember coming from my parents. The only time ever imposed was "be home before dark" when we played in the streets.

"You'll know when". Little did she know the struggle that her thirteen year old had in making the decision! Finally, I resolved my dilemma by using Walter's schedule. Walter was a man who boarded at our home. He left for work at 11 pm. That sounded like a good time for me to return home.

Years later, was the same loose discipline in effect? My younger sibling was now the 7th grader. He seemed not to be under the before dark rule. In fact he was a bit unruly. He had made friends a tad too old for him, had run away to Ohio with them and was soon returned by the police . . . . I wonder if it was before dark.

He had developed a behavior more consistent with returning home after dark. My mom would stretch out on the sofa awaiting his safe arrival home. As he entered she would feign sleep and through guarded eye openings peek to see what he was up to. She shared his ritual with me. He would arrive after 10 pm, open a bottle of Nehi orange pop, light up a cigarette and kind of hang loose for the time it took to ingest his Nehi drink and smoke.

When he completed his pleasure routine, he would empty the ash try and wipe down any remnants of the 10 cent Nehi orange drink and cigarette that might remain on the end table.

And so it continued—his after dark rituals, her motherly surveillance—with no discipline following. How long?

Eighth grade. A conversion took place. Perhaps it was gradual. I am not sure if my mother saw it happening. But she rejoiced when her son received the American Legion Award for outstanding leadership and citizenship at his graduation. The Medal of Honor replaced the 10 cent Nehi orange and cigarette ritual.

How different was the Judas story where his after dark events did not allow for a gradual conversion. One hopeless attempt, one act of despair! There would be no rejoicing.

Judas was reclining at table with Jesus and the other chosen eleven. It was Passover. Perhaps it was when his brother disciples had prepared for this meal of observance that Judas had slipped away to make other preparations, plans with the chief priests and scribes.

Now Jesus prays the Kiddush. He begins: Barukh atah Adonai, Eloheinu, melekh ha'olam—Blessed are you, Lord, our God, sovereign of the universe . . .

Judas is there with a money bag filled with 30 pieces of silver. As they were eating, Jesus spoke of betrayal: "Amen, amen, I say to you, one of you will betray me". No name was mentioned. But to Judas he said: "What you are going to do, do quickly". No reprimand, no discipline were imposed.

What was Judas going to do? Jesus knew but did not interfere. Judas left at once. And it was night. The others did not suspect that the money bag Judas held was a part of a plan, a money ritual to be fulfilled still later . . . in the Garden of Olives.

Judas went there—his companions came carrying swords and clubs. Judas was armed with a kiss. The ritual deed was done, carried out after dark.

The aftermath of this night left Judas trying to recant his deed. He attempted to "clean up" the evidence, to return the 30 coins. They were not accepted. His failed conversion attempt left Judas hopeless.

A rope, a place in Potters Field—these replaced the 30 pieces of silver.

20

Chicken Soup is Good

Chicken soup is good". The recipe has been uttered by our moms ad infinitum. It is as though it were the archetype for recovery to good health, inbred in those named "mother". I suppose the advice was a special gift given to them, those who would be called to be nurturers. It was never in competition with the apple, the recipe fruit that failed to meet the expectation of our first mom. Nor does the simplicity of 'drink plenty of water'—good old H20—'to remain healthy' fit the standard.

Nurturing is a female thing, isn't it? My dad never suggested chicken soup as a cure all for ills. His idea of good soup was ox tail prepared by him. For what purpose but to please his palate! My mom refused to make it. We kids never experimented with it—even under pain of mortal sin.

Chicken soup even emerged in book stores. "Chicken Soup for . . ." books were presented as recipes in the various relationships common to us all. In their way they have become another version of the original archetype.

"Chicken Soup for . . ." books have reached out to bring messages that will nurture our whole being. Open a cover and life pours out with shared stories of hope, courage, inspiration, relationships and love.

One Christmas, I gave a copy of the book to a teen relative. I think it was one of the books about teens. I was surprised by her delight with the gift. At the same time I discovered another reason that chicken soup is good. This girl is an athlete and sports and high school requirements consume her time leaving a bit less for other reading. She enjoys "Chicken Soup for . . ." because of its messages and the style, the individual stories. They engage her and allow her time to sneak a peek and not have to pursue three hundred pages to discover an ending. The series continues to invite her interests and to lead her to bookstores or libraries to enjoy reading.

But beyond reading this girl is personally health conscious for self and others and enters walks to promote health concerns. As she continues on, her journey—her wish, is to become a dietician. Chicken Soup is for her reading but seems not for the traditional mom's recipe for her health.

To the compilers of the series, a thought—"Chicken Soup for the Soul: A Thirst for Reading!

No one offered him chicken soup as he hung from the cross. Instead, they satisfied his call for water, his thirst, with vinegar. The word vinegar comes from the French word "vinagre" which means "sour wine".

Ancients probably discovered it accidently when their wines fermented. Hippocrates prescribed vinegar as a remedy for a variety of ailments. Scripture reveals that Boaz allows Ruth to dip a piece of bread in the vinegar. The Prophet Muhammad called it a "blessed seasoning". Today, people are using it in hundreds of different ways—from cooking and cleaning to gardening and the laundry.

But the soldiers, his crucifiers, what did they intend when this "vinegar" was brushed against Jesus' lips and pressed into his mouth? A blessing? A remedy? We think the worst since our experience of a sip of vinegar offers a bitter bite. Scripture does not reveal Jesus' response except that he had cried out: "I thirst!"

Were there healing properties in that vinegar? Or was his need satisfied even by that bitter offering?

Where was the baptismal water that was poured over him in the Jordan? Where were the vats of water that were turned into good wine? Where the tears of the sinful woman that fell on the feet of Jesus?

We recall how Jesus met a Samarian woman at a well. We may glean in his conversation with her something about that well water, what it is for those who thirst. "Everyone who drinks of this water will be thirsty again."

The soldiers offered Jesus vinegar not well water. They pierced him with a spear and blood and water flowed from his side. Did those actions belong to the mystery of Jesus' words to the woman—"Whoever drinks the water I will give will never thirst"? A Jesus h20!

A prayerful offering—Chicken Soup for the Soul: A Thirst for Your "H20", Jesus!

24

Matthew's Foggy Mountain.

Memorial Day weekend—no Friday Ethics class today. So Matthew and I planned to meet not on a mountain but in my 12th floor residence. It was here that we actually continued a trip that began when he was a college student at ECC City. and rambled though his final graduation and teaching degree.

I invited Matthew to a youth experience held monthly called Theology on Tap. Each experience led us to many after presentation talks to Tim Horton's and a continuation of the topic. We were both disappointed when the series of talks was discontinued. However, Matthew became interested in joining me for the weekly philosophy class that I was taking. His interest was peeked and his desire to talk about each class offering led us once more to Tim Horton's and an hour of post class discussion.

On this particular Friday a now 24 year old and an xx ol' nun would get together to chat—not about theology or philosophy. Rather we met to chat about our common interest in and activity of writing. It was kind of like our TH experiences together. Here on the heights of my 12th floor "mountain" Matthew shared the vivid truth of the person he had become. He shared stories of his many trips that were handwritten in a red notebook since he was thirteen years old—the notebook given him by his father. Each December 31st it recorded the top three events of the past year.

The evening revealed his favorite view of the vista from a foggy mountain. Even more, the written and shared remembrances exposed just who Matthew had become. Here in my view was a young man totally open to the many life opportunities of a yet to be discovered trip ahead of him—places to visit, discoveries to be opened. curiosity to be answered and an urgency to continue his life adventure. "I want my spirit to be open even when my body grows old" he shared. And, he continued "I have a question for God. I want to know your plan for me". In the meantime, Matthew is looking forward to continuing his "trip".

The evening came to a close when he peeked over my shoulder to read the episode in my second book called "Ethni-city" where his name was mentioned as being president of the Campus Ministry Association. He responded with excitement that I had included his name "Matthew"—"Wow! It made my night!"

Well, the truth be told Matthew made my night!

The scene was a mountain top. Jesus had invited Peter, John and James to join him there to pray. Soon something happened there. Moses and Elijah appeared "in glory" and Jesus was having a chat with them. It was about Jesus' death and how it would be accomplished in Jerusalem. Did Peter and his companions, covered by a cloud, hear what they were observing? Perhaps not. But, they were afraid when they saw that Jesus' face changed and his clothing became brilliant as lightening. What they did hear was a voice revealing "this is my Son, the Chosen One. Listen to him". Their response was silence. They told no one.

There was so much mystery surrounding this mountain experience. Eight days earlier Jesus had spoken about the kingdom and the question posed was directed to Peter: Who do you say that I Am?" When Peter responded "the Christ of God", Jesus ordered him to tell no one about this.

Peter was charged with silence two times. Yet later when he has an opportunity to speak up, what does he do? Do we hear his words—"I do not know him"?

Peter was privileged to experience the transfiguration of Christ, the revelation of the Son of God. On his journey he would eventually break the silence, and he would even make up for his denials. It would be the gift of the Holy Spirit at Pentecost when he would follow Christ's directive to go out to the world and proclaim the good news!

Peter's Father gave him no red notebook to mark his foggy mountain experience. Rather he gave him a role to play as Rock and a cross to proclaim salvation. Thus Peter's final days as a disciple of the risen Christ is his story of a trip to the mountain with it's vista reaching into the present and leading the way to God's kingdom.

25
Unopened Gifts

When I discovered "Monk" on TV, I rushed home after Friday evening classes to watch what became one of my favorites. Perhaps my attachment to the show was akin to Monk's obsessive compulsions—mine, a need to see each episode and some more than once.

The story line for each episode focused on a current crime, Monk's relationship with his psychiatrist as he attempted to work out his excessive compulsive behavior, and always, with his struggle to deal with his late wife's death. Trudy Monk was killed, murdered when she was going on an errand.

In the last two episodes Monk was reminded again of Trudy as he fondled an unopened gift. When he was convinced that he should open the gift there was an unexpected revelation. It was a video prepared by Trudy with a message that exposed the truth about her murder, pointed to the killer and offered a still greater gift for Monk.

One day, Eddy became my Monk. This fellow, a wonderful husband to my cousin and father to their three children is not Catholic. He grew up in a home where the family faith was Evangelical Christian. I did not know anything about his faith commitment but I knew he wasn't Catholic.

When I was invited to a Christmas gathering, my non Catholic in-law came to my mind and I timidly prepared to make a suggestion about his faith. Thus it was that I wrapped a gift for him, a small book introducing the beliefs of the catholic faith. I carried my gift to the Christmas get together and all the while butterflies tingled inside me. How does one present such a gift? Providence offered the first opportunity. As we gathered waiting for our Santa to hand out our gifts, Eddy sat to my right. While others were chatting away, I turned to him, handed him the gift and whispered my message: "Your kids are all baptized Catholic; you faithfully attend Mass with your family, so I want to give you this gift. Open this when you wish and I will be happy to help you if you choose to prepare yourself".

What happens when, in the midst of much chatting, someone whispers to another? The room became silent. From the other side of the room, his wife called out: "Ruu . . . thyy". I did not reveal the nature of the gift although his wife must have caught part of my message.

I left the gathering that December 25th day leaving this special little gift behind, yet unopened-. unopened among those that filled the room with all the kid's toys and their adult exchanges. What happened later? I don't know if Eddy was eager to take a peek or if he set it aside, as did Monk, perhaps for another day. What Eddy does not know is, like Monk, what a treasure that book truly reveals. I am left wondering if he still fondles his gift . . . does it remain on a shelf. Or has he opened the gift to take a peek?

Do you think Jesus might have experienced the tingle of butterflies that day when he was in his home town? In other towns he visited he performed many mighty deeds. Here in his own town, they wondered about Jesus as he was teaching in the synagogue. The people—his neighbors—took offense at him. Why? Because he was no one special—a carpenter, son of Mary with relatives and friends there in Nazareth!

Jesus offered a reason" "A prophet is not without honor except in his native place and among his own kin and in his house." Jesus was saying, in effect, that those closest to you do not have the same respect for the gifts you bring. He was amazed at their lack of faith. It was because of that lack of faith in him that the people did not receive the gifts, the mighty deeds, Jesus had to offer.

It is like the Monk story. Monk so clung to the memories of the past, the stories of life with Trudy told over and again that he left her gift unopened. Seasons of Monk passed with viewers struggling with Monk's reality while a box remained on his shelf. In the end, the revelation Trudy offered was her mighty gift— a treasure of love and healing for Monk.

And Eddy? In the home of our family, among close relatives— my kin, there came a cry of disbelief. No one asked for the gift to be opened because it was from a relative, a "home towner", cousin Ruthy.

28

Extreme Makeover-Home Destruction

The Queen City offered a November greeting to the bus carrying the crew from the "Extreme Makeover-Home Edition" show. Snow was saved for other days. Instead, a Buffalo November offered a week of blue skies and sunny days to its visitors.

Five thousand volunteers—west side neighbors, Buffalonians from other parts of the city and suburbanites donned in white helmets and blue shirts—invaded Massachusetts Street, a living evidence of our "City of Good Neighbors" reputation. They would construct a house proper to the vernacular of the area and would include a neighbor-friendly front porch. The new home was to be a prototype for an urban Buffalo home, one that fit in a narrow lot. In the end, it was lauded as a designer, architectural and good neighbor success.

Perhaps as they looked at the empty living room they remembered a Brooklyn apartment, in the rear of the main house, the place they had called home briefly. To enter one had to open a side door of a two story house, walk through the basement, open a door at the end to what they would call home—kitchen and living area, a bedroom and bath. Perhaps its fondest memory was that it was here where their first child was born, and here where Lori often even entertained late night guests with a wonderful spread.

On a snowy January 28th, the birthday of a common friend, we had gathered in this, new, unfinished home to celebrate. We crowded into the kitchen for gift giving and cake. Aha! Cake! It was I who had created this cake with affection for the celebrant. But, it was not I who complained out loud, "the cake is tooo dry!"

What happened next was due to Lori's urging. It was Lori, the new woman of the house that incited the cake war that followed in her new home. Why had she posed such a challenging question: "What does that make you feel like doing?" I knew and I made the first toss. Others joined the war and cake decorated people, and yes, the clean walls and floors of this new house. Children cried and the dog barked. Then, the war went out the front door. Frosting now mixed with snow as Frank and I ran to blast more cake on the one who had called, "dry!"

The cake war was one of frivolity played out among family and friends gathered to celebrate. We heard two sounds . . . first were strains of "happy birthday" and then a single word—"dry!"

Scripture reveals Jesus in situations played out during his time in Jerusalem. There was no frivolity here. Jesus knew the seriousness of coming to Jerusalem and the concerns of the disciples. But he did not heed their warnings.

Jesus was entering Jerusalem, this place for his final celebration. The atmosphere did not anticipate what might be sorrowful. Rather it was filled with shouts of "Hosanna" and palms were waved in his honor. Shortly after the arrival, his disciples went to find a house where he might celebrate the Jewish Passover, a last supper.

It was in this atmosphere of celebrations that Jesus visited the temple, the place he called his "house"—"My house shall be called a house of prayer." Yet, gathered in his house were moneychangers and some selling doves. There was buying and selling going on. Where were the hosannas now, the prayer and the honor due the One who dwelt there? There were "thieves" in his house, defiling its call to holiness.

And Jesus reacted. Tables and chairs were overturned. Jesus, in a kind of war, was throwing the "thieves" out of the house, chasing them away.

There was a war 'in the beginning too. Remember how Satan and his den of disturbers were cast out of God's house? Maybe we can see ourselves in the scene, helpful, entering his war and tossing out the disturbers, casting out Satan and his evil ways even from our lives.

Jesus had also made a promise: "In my Father's house there are many rooms." We will enter, not disturbers, not deconstructing those holy places. We will enter the rooms readied for us—not as thieves but as those who have kept his will.

I pause and recreate a memory of the scene in Lori's new house. There's no maybe about our presence and participation—we were the disturbers, the ones deconstructing what had not yet even been completed. The living room would be completed another day, readied and inviting for other friendship celebrations.

71

Water, Water... Everywhere?

It was January. I was accompanying students—four boys and a girl, in our Campus Ministry stance for life—to participate in the walk for life on the anniversary of Roe vs. Wade.

Washington D.C. offered us a frigid welcome. In addition to our bus arriving too late for the Bishop's greeting, I had a meeting with the sidewalk. The boys had removed the scooter from the bus and I perched on it to begin my ride into the gathering room. In an unexpected move, I was on the ground. In another swift move two of the boys lifted me from my helpless position. They became my guards protecting me on my scooter from any possible fall as I rode along joining the mass of marchers.

I was helpless on that sidewalk. Yet, I was fortunate to have someone come to my rescue. How ironic that I was in this place to participate in another rescue attempt, to challenge a Supreme Court decision that prevented the rescue of babies from their helpless position, babies confronted by the tools of disregard for their life.

There was another day, several years earlier, when Washington D.C. welcomed another Campus Ministry group. We were a party of college students and staff there to participate in a July gathering to proclaim our reverence for life. The July heat absorbed our energy but our focus was on the speakers who engaged us. We sat among the mass of people who gathered as a sign of protest against Roe vs. Wade.

We came to witness to our belief. We came to proclaim being pro-life. We came to be fed.

On this earlier trip I had had no need for a scooter. But soon the need that arose was for water. Water stations had been placed all over the area. Yet, as we approached them, one by one we were turned away. The masses of people had consumed all the available water. Water covers 71% of the Earth's surface, and is vital for all known forms of life. Water everywhere on Earth, except here in Washington! Here there was not a drop to drink!

Finally a rescue! The Smithsonian Museum offered us the comfort of a shield from the heat and drinks to quench our temporary thirst.

Two trips separated by years but focused on our pro life stance and efforts! Each presented a helplessness that called out for a rescue. Each received a response to the need. Thanks to those rescuers!

———————————

How many times do we read in scripture that someone was helpless—one was sitting on the edge of a healing pool unable to go in by himself; another was lifted up on his mat by caregivers to present him to the healer. These and others were rescued from their helplessness. They were healed and offered the gift of life.

Remember the woman that Jesus met at the well? She came to find relief for her thirst. She came to Jacob's well, that special well where Jacob himself and his family and flocks drank from. She came when the noon day heat was creating her need for a drink. Water! Yes there was water for her comfort. But Jesus offered her something more—to feed her with living water, water that would become for her "eternal life".

Those two campus ministry trips and the helplessness we experienced bring to mind those actions of Jesus—rescuing those whose need is . . . to be lifted up, to drink, to live. They bring to mind our role in rescuing the unborn who lie on the mat of a mother's womb and offering them . . . life.

129

Breaking the Binkie Habit

Babies have a natural urge to suck. Binkies, blankets and thumbs are common outlets for that natural urge. Most will discontinue the habit of non nutritive sucking between the ages of two and four.

But what happens if the child continues beyond four and fails to yield to the power of the pacifier, continues sucking away—say into the first experience of school, into pre-K?

The professional answer offered is called "staging". The recommendation is to change the behavior, to allow using the binkie progressively harder. Praise, positive reinforcement, promises—three Ps! One or more of these approaches may work to stop the sucking say professionals.

But there is no magic bullet to breaking the habit. My mom knew that well although I am not sure she had used one or any of the 3 Ps.

I remember my pre-K brother and his binkie—we just dubbed it by its appearance—a "nipple". The important part was that his was attached to a bottle and apparently sucked so long that it had lost its new small shape and taken on some comforting shape. I doubt that it was the same bottle-binkie that pacified him way back when.

Often times his binkie would be dropped somewhere and our search began amid his loud cries. My mom's promise of a new one did not quell the storm of tears. His insistence was for the same one, shaped for his pleasure . . . And when found was washed for reuse.

Now it happened that one day the boy tossed his bottle from our backyard residence at 127 with its precious nipple into the neighbor's back yard. Worse, the family at 129 had a chicken coop. The precious binkie, bottle and, all landed in that small chicken coop near our fence. His cries insisted that mom get it and she insisted that the chicken had eaten it. His solution was to cut the chicken to retrieve it.

But I think that was the end of the popular bottle-binkie habit—a "cold turkey" experience.

Did the disciples absolutely give up fishing to follow Jesus? After all they were fishermen at heart and trade. We know that Simon and Andrew were casting their nets into the sea, that James and John were in a boat mending their nets when they heard: "Come after me and I will make you fishers of men." Yes, they left their nets and followed him and left their boats along with hired men.

I think of scenes when Jesus was on a boat with the disciples or when he called out to them from the shore. We are reminded how they had spent the night but caught nothing. From amid what must have been shouts of dismay, the frustrated disciples hear Jesus give them an instruction that results in their huge catch.

What of the scene when the storm breaks while disciples are on a boat and Jesus wakes to quell the storm?

What do those scenes suggest? Did they have the urge to return to the sea at times? After all, other scenes have them occupied in the company of Jesus and growing into a new habit—one of discipleship, of becoming fishers of men.

Might scenes like these have been opportunities for Jesus to teach his three Ps—praise, positive reinforcement, promises—for the road he was asking them to follow?

Were his 3 Ps simply signs, offered in "stages" and leading to the end of their old fishing habit?

275

Old Frames

The post card sized picture is fitted snugly in a blue frame, a frame marked with scratches etched there by age. It stands on a shelf in front of some spiritual books (and even one called Raccota, a book of Indulgences). Three smile as they lean on a patio railing probably in response to a camera man's call: "say cheese". It was a spring day of a spring relationship. Kathy, me, Pat, and behind the camera—Dick.

We were a motley group of four who had first met over coffee in a Campus Ministry setting at City Campus. A Campus Minister, a math professor, a secretary and a maintenance man, we soon wore a cap simply called 'friends'. That title brought us together for sharing things like Friday dinners and birthday celebrations and visits to each others' homes. Of course those early morning coffees together continued in the college frame of Room 275.

And nearby, out of sight of that camera, outside of that picture, but frequently a part of our times together, were husband Hank, baseball fan mom Bubby, and dear, shy, Mary Lee another math guru at the college.

The scratched blue frame reminds me that many years have passed since a last gathering. Reminds me that many have left the college and our foursome! 2000 and two had already retired. When? 2007 another leaves and one remains on Campus. So, now it is 2010 and long past that once season of friendship and into the winter season blanketing the spring memories and experiences and that foursome friendship.

I was reminded recently that friendships change and what once was becomes something different. Sometimes there is an end. Who even knew that 'Kath girl', Pat, Dick and Sis Ruth were friends? Who remembers when we visited last, when the drifting away began? Ended?

What lingers is the joy captured in those smiling faces in that old blue frame recording one day in the springtime of a friendship.

We are reminded of a motley group of twelve who walked along with Jesus. He had called them away from other tasks to share a special friendship. Their times together are captured in four old frames—gospels which portray them in the springtime of their relationship. Like photos in an album, their faces emerge to reveal times together.

Now we see the picture of twelve framed in the Passover meal with their friend, the one they called Master. It is a last meal together. We see young John and notice the glow of being a special friend. Philip is there, perhaps with the same wonder on his face as when he stood before Jesus with a few fish to feed so many. There is a wishful look on James and John who still want to sit at Jesus' left and right in the kingdom. Thomas once called this Jesus, "God", yet there is a gloom in his appearance. And Peter—there is a look of anticipation that marks his demeanor. Judas has a guilty look about him. The other six have a tired look as when they had hauled in the many fish after a night of empty nets.

Twelve gathered to share a meal. Did they even suspect it was the last Passover meal together? A last time on their journey with Jesus and with their companions? Jesus looked into the faces, into the expressions of his friends as they gathered at the table. He saw in them how these men would finally respond to their three years of companionship together.

Now they would leave this place and each would await the promise of Jesus—the fullness of the Spirit, that they would emerge wearing new caps called "fishers of men". Scripture presents the picture of that Pentecost experience, their last group experience. Now what lingers in the old frame of memories changes as each departs, goes out "into the whole world to teach the good News".

Today, there is a remnant of a one time group of four friends—changed, responding to individual calls, wearing new caps that invite them to new experiences, somewhere in the world.

575

Tit for Tat

John was a daily visitor, a long time colleague and friend, a business professor, retired cop and a faithful catholic. It was as that catholic that he emerged from his room 575 office, that he sauntered along the corridor to his on campus favorite coffee haunt—Campus Ministry—with an offer. "If I sell my house I will buy Campus Ministry a new computer!" Now who could refuse that offer—tit for tat? I quickly reminded him of the tradition of burying a statue of St. Joseph, and saying the proper prayer to encourage the sale.

Why St. Joseph? He is known as the patron of real estate matters and home sales. A logical tribute because he was a carpenter who taught Jesus the trade and always saw that Jesus was well housed. How long this saint cult legend goes back is not certain. But, my catholic friend accepted the claim and wanted in! At his bidding I sought out a statue and the prayer.

Directions:

1. *Make a hole in the ground that is large enough to bury the St. Joseph statue (in protective wrap).*
2. *Place the statue upside down in the ground.*
3. *Face the upside down statue TOWARDS the home that is to be sold.*
4. *For nine consecutive days, pray the St. Joseph Novena.*
5. *Once the home is sold, remove the statue from the ground.*
6. *Display the statue in a place of honor in the new home.*

Then, offer the novena prayer which begins:

O, Saint Joseph, you who taught our Lord the carpenter's trade, and saw to it that he was always properly housed, hear my earnest plea. I want you to help me now as you helped your foster-child Jesus, and as you have ped many others in the matter of housing. wish to sell this [house/property] quickly, easily, and profitably and I implore you to grant my wish by bringing me a good buyer, one who is eager, compliant, and honest, and by letting nothing impede the rapid conclusion of the sale.

What can be said of turning to saints for mediation or a faithful catholic seeking the mediation of his Campus Minister and the recommended house selling adjunct—Joseph?

The offer was tit for tat. For John, his response, his gift came even before the house was sold. But, Joseph did his thing . . . just a bit later.

Does Jesus ever respond tit for tat? The question I posed did not linger long or unanswered. I pictured the scene. Jesus had entered the Pharisee's house and reclined at table. A sinful woman is criticized for anointing him with her tears and kisses. Jesus forgives the woman her sins. Then immediately he teaches about forgiveness and love. The question is posed to his host about two debtors being forgiven. Which would love more? The one to whom little is forgiven, loves little. Thus, the woman whose many sins are forgiven loves more. Tit for tat?

Another scene comes to mind. The woman was surrounded by those who accused her of adultery. They stand ready to stone her to death for her sin. Jesus bends down and writes in the sand. Why do the accusers drop their stones? What are the words that make them leave? Tit for tat?

Like the statue of Joseph that is placed below the ground surface wrapped in our faith, I think there is a tit for tat that emerges from many of the stories, the parables of Jesus.

On the other hand, we might consider his simple responses: render to Caesar what is Caesar's and to God what belongs to God; or, no miracles could be performed in his home town because of their disbelief.

We approach the stories, the interactions of Jesus with those who call out in faith looking for the "offers" among the scriptural reminders. We may also seek them through the mediators, the tradition of saints, and the people we meet on our way.

Those tit for tat offers are available to us . . . if we but saunter through scripture or tradition or even down a hall and over a cup of coffee.

638

The Watchmaker's Shop

Hertel Avenue is like a tree whose trunk stretches from the shores of the Towpath Park and Niagara River to Main Street. Along the long trunk there are many important branches—other avenues and streets that run south toward the inner city and north or south to outlying suburbs. Others simply end in the many areas that mark them as North Buffalo and some in its northwest corner known as the old historical Black Rock area.

It is not unusual for me to leave my home near the Tow Path to travel via that trunk to my destinations. Nor is it unusual for me to glance to the left, to notice the bold, clearly displayed numbers—638. The place has looked vacant for a long time. As I wonder if the shop is actually occupied, my mind drifts to other moments, times when a watchmaker spent his free hours there.

My dad had an avocation, indeed a passion, for repairing watches. As long as I could remember he had his watchmaker's bench in our home. His was a generation without TV. I think the bench and his task provided an important respite after a long day working at Curtis Wright or Bell Aircraft as a draftsman. Instead of reclining with a remote in one hand, a beer in the other, dad leaned forward at his bench both hands tending to the watch parts before him. Both hands were doing the delicate surgery required to clean, repair or replace the brokenness of a watch.

As I look back, I remember first as an only child spending late afternoons or Saturdays just watching and offering him a kid's company, some quiet quality time with my dad at home. Later as a teen, when for a brief period dad's bench found its way to the shop on Hertel Ave. I too found my way to that place via a bus ride with a transfer to 638 to continue to share precious daughter-dad time.

Watches continued to fail and my watchmaker dad continued to restore them. But at some unremembered time there was no longer our 638, nor a bench in our home. The time came for change. Broken watches were tossed away and replaced at a store. Arthritic hands yielded the watchmakers task to new tasks. The one who had taken the random parts of a watch strewn on his bench and put them back together was in a recliner holding a remote in one hand and a beer in the other.

The child who had shared many childhood hours with her watchmaker dad also changed with the times. No longer his bench with the quality time! Today, a too late thought—what did I miss by not sharing a beer with my retired watchmaker dad?

The book of Genesis reveals that in the beginning there was chaos and out of that chaos God spoke and by his word created all that he would finally call "good".

There have been, and are, many who claimed there is no God at all. Theologians and philosophers through the centuries have proposed arguments to prove the existence of God.

William Paley was an Anglican theologian born in the middle of the 18th century. He proposed a theory, an argument from design as a proof for the existence of God. It is called a teleological argument—one based on the design and purpose of the natural world.

Paley makes his argument using the analogy of "the Watchmaker". Simply, his argument is for intelligent design and goes something like this:

If you found a watch in a field, next to a stone, you would conclude that it was an artifact, that it was designed by someone . . . a watchmaker. It was not formed randomly.

In the same way, when we look at life and the universe and how they operate we see how perfectly and orderly they function.

We can easily conclude that, like the parts of a watch, all of creation with its parts belongs to a whole, a whole with an intelligent designer. And, because of the vast complexity of the universe there must be a vastly intelligent designer who created it.

Theologians will cite differences or disagreements with it. But I can admit of Paley's argument. Why? It is because I have seen the parts of a watch strewn on a watchmaker's bench. And I knew that watchmaker who put them in order and called it "good".

1967
The Letter

I tore open the letter anxious to explore the content information. A rush came over me as I read words like "accepted" . . . "postulant" . . . "September". The good news had arrived and I would soon begin my journey as a Grey Nun. It would begin as a postulant and the entry date was the feast of Our Lady, September 8th.1967.

The first person to hear my good news was my friend Sheila. Immediately, she proclaimed that her entry gift to me would be a black rosary. Now what remained was how to tell my parents and family.

May provided a good time since the family would be gathered to celebrate Mother's Day and my birthday. So a plan emerged on how to share the news, news not expected by those gathered.

Since I would be receiving birthday gifts, our plan was to have Sheila's gift be the last. I would open her gift and find a black rosary and a picture of Marguerite d'Youville. That would allow me to explain the twin gift as my life changing choice to enter the Grey Nuns.

Simple, right! Well an earlier gift from a brother was a crystal rosary. Oops! When he saw the black one he admired it and even said he'd return the crystal one. The question rose—"Why black?"

Why black? Now I was able to share an important event in my life with those closest to me. There were happy greetings and questions about my choice raised with simple curiosity and affirmation.

Soon I realized my dad was not in the room. I tracked him down to the basement where he was hunched over a repair bench working on one of the watches—its parts strewn on the bench top. Repairing watches was my dad's avocation and his alone time. It was like he could sort out his thoughts just as he sorted the parts of a watch and come up with the right end. Was he sorting out this decision by his daughter, trying to get the pieces of my life in an understandable order?

I don't remember the words but tears were in his eyes. They were happy tears, and I realized they were his quiet admission of joy for my choice. They were, like for so many other choices I made, the unspoken acceptance saying it's ok. Often I heard of his pride in me through others. So there was no reason for a spoken "ok" to say he was proud of me that day.

Jesus made a decision. He would go to Jerusalem and there fulfill his life's journey. We picture his entry: people gathered to welcome him. They cheered his arrival and waved palm branches, their unspoken acceptance of this man, recognizing his reputation for healing and concern for the underprivileged. They had heard the stories. Now they dignified his presence as he arrived. Yes, Jesus' reputation outside of Jerusalem had followed him to this day of entry—this day we call Palm Sunday,

His friends arrived with him but had discouraged his choice to enter Jerusalem. Why?

Out of the sight of the cheering crowd and the waving palms, other plans were being hatched. They could be traced to the priests and the Roman officials who did not want their roles undermined by this itinerant preacher. Here in Jerusalem. Among those who had welcomed him, there was a quiet conspiracy going on. It was played out in the Temple and the Roman Praetorium by groups that failed to acknowledge him. The priests charged Jesus with blasphemy and the state officials with uprising and calling himself king.

Jerusalem. The choice was made. It was his good news for the people. Yet, that very news caused some to enter the basement of their arenas of concern, to sort out what they must do. There in their temple and in their Praetorium, their conspiracy, their self pride would be their response . . . not to accept Jesus' good news.

Nuns are People Too . . .

Just take a peek and see

"Why do you seek the living among the dead?"

Flying Nun Project

1990

8

Keys

Many of us have had the experience of fumbling in a purse or coat pocket looking for a key, the right key for its particular entry—usually a house key, or a car door or engine key. Perhaps the sought after key opens a mailbox. It's a task that is particularly difficult when hands are occupied holding something or when light is a premium.

I have enjoyed using a lanyard with each key placed in an order that is comfortable for me to find.

As I swung my lanyard to reach the key that opened my apartment door, my thoughts swung back to a novitiate experience and keys that opened other doors.

Eight o'clock had drawn us into the community room for the traditional recreation hour anonymously dubbed "forced fun". This evening there was something celebrative about our gathering. The senior novices would be leaving the Novitiate, the Grey Nun Motherhouse, for their first mission assignment. They had planned this hour as a kind of graduation ceremony. As part of this departure event, there was a tradition of handing down responsibilities—their last will and testament.

Among the hand me downs were two keys. One opened the door to our designated, though unofficial clinic. The other opened the door to the medicine cabinet where an array of all the unscripted remedies filled its shelves. The holder of these keys was a kind of pharmacist nun. She was able to dole out over the counter pills and other physical soothers.

The surprise was that the keys of that kingdom were willed to me by Dawn. During her reign as pharmacist nun Dawn was held in high regard. That regard extended into all aspects of her three year Novitiate experiences.

Now, keys entrusted to me? Was this hand-me-down responsibility an honor or a challenge?

How ironic that keys that were used for opening somehow belonged to a time of closing. Yet, at that time there was an unknown future for Dawn and keys and another opening. Years later, at this writing, Dawn was offered other keys—a role of service, a call to be a member of the congregation's leadership team.

We pray with Jesus: "Thy Kingdom come . . . on earth as it is in Heaven." Jesus came, aware of his role as Savior. He knew that he had the keys to the kingdom, keys that would open the doors of heaven—for those who had already fallen asleep and for each of us.

Jesus began his role when he was thirty three and his term of service, his ministry—his novitiate, as it were—ended three years later when he celebrated an end to his earthly life. But his gift, his kingdom would not die on that Cross.

"On earth as it is in Heaven", we pray. Before Jesus would make a final earthly departure he had promised the disciples that he would not leave them alone. What were the hand-me-down responsibilities—his will and testament that would be his promise to remain with them, with us?

Jesus called Peter "rock" and upon the rock he promised to build his Church.

Jesus said, *"And I will give you the keys of the Kingdom of Heaven: and whatsoever you shall bind on earth shall be bound in Heaven: and whatsoever you shall loose on earth shall be loosed in Heaven."* Matt 16:19

Peter received the keys—his role as leader of the Church on earth. There came a day when he passed on that responsibility and when each holder of the keys thereafter passed on that tradition, that commission set in motion by Jesus—his will and testament to his Church.

11

Day Spices and Night Riders

I hobbled into my new assignment on a broken leg. My arrival there returned the number of sisters in the house, a convent in Queens back to nine. One sister had left and I was the new replacement.

It was a welcoming community and my third assignment as a junior professed sister. The first two had each been one semester teaching experiences. Now in the New York area I would become familiar with a whole new group of professed sisters—eight teaching sisters—one among them a convent superior and last but not least, the sister cook.

They say variety is the spice of life. Our community of nine was filled with spice! There were the gaming sisters—three enjoyed evenings gathering together to play board games. Another was ready to offer help, to do my wash which required a trip to the basement; a difficult task in my one leg condition (arrived donned with a cast). Still another assured me that if I would be the driver on her trips to local stores "you will soon learn your way around New York". Then there was the wonderful sister-cook. Her meals were outstanding. Best of all was her bread pudding. But after she discovered I picked away the raisins, she would gently point out a non raisin corner of the pudding that she saved for me. Yes, the place was full of spice! I became comfortable with my new home and with life in the school as well. A visit by the school principal on Tuesdays was as our dinner guest and as my tutor—my tutor since I knew nothing about the arithmetic now dubbed modern math.

From out of this setting, there came an unexpected invitation. One of our sisters would leave the house shortly after school was out. This daily routine was never spoken of aloud. Then one day she approached me and asked a favor. Perhaps I was selected when she noticed I kept late hours. Most others were already asleep while I indulged in corn flakes and warm milk—a late night snack alone in the kitchen. Would I be willing to pick her up at 11 pm from a designated address? My yes did not seek any information nor was any offered. We became night riders until one night she no longer needed my help.

Then we became eight sisters.

Career changes are common. They are born out of discernment and response to social conditions, education, personal gifts and interests. It happens among people in all walks of life. For one involved, change might be expressed as personal and private.

My thoughts wandered into scripture. Remember that Jesus left home when he was around 30. He had been reared in a small town and in the home of a carpenter and had been a carpenter himself. Then the change came when he left home and became an itinerant preacher.

As he entered this new way of life, did you ever wonder why he chose fishermen to follow him? Why not carpenters? He told each that that he would be a fisher of men. Was Jesus really intending to use a cliché or a pun? Was he being funny?

Nevertheless, those fishermen joined him although they apparently knew little about him or where he lived. They never asked many questions. It was Jesus who made his invitation clear, set the directions they must follow.

Who would follow a man who could not promise them a place to lay their head? Yet soon enough they became a community of disciples, twelve men willing to change their lives, to leave the comfort of their former lives to follow him.

I was one junior professed who moved into a community of nine. They were twelve disciples who were entering the mystery of One whom they would call Master, Teacher. They listened as he presented the new way—the law is made for man, not man for the law. They were introduced to new behaviors based on love—turning the cheek, forgiving, offering your coat . . .

Even among the convent group of nine changes might happen. Vatican II called sisters to discern their call of service. What was the discernment here? I look back on a sister who quietly discerned a new call for her life.

But scripture tells of a disciple—one whose discernment was an unholy alliance that would lead him to even ending his life.

It happened one evening at a supper, one disciple left the table. He had some coins and a night job to complete—to identify Jesus from among the other disciples who had gathered to pray. In the cover of night there was a kiss.

Then they became eleven disciples.

13

!n Search of a Fat Girls' Store

When you are overweight—nun or not—the search for clothes may require an unfamiliar journey. So it was that we were on the road to Germantown a neighborhood in northwest Philadelphia.

Among its claims as a neighborhood rich in historic sites and buildings from the colonial era, I was informed that there was a store that specialized in "fat girl clothes". Thirteen Quaker and Mennonite families founded the area. Now six Catholic nuns were crowded into a car in search of that "specialty" store located in this original German settlement.

I wanted to buy a bathing suit. I am not sure now if my co-passenger nuns drove along for the ride or if they had an interest in making a purchase as well. In preparation for having to try on any selection, I chose not to wear my veil for the event.

I was the driver of the car—one from our Motherhouse—where we had gathered for a congregational meeting. Now in Germantown approaching the specified area, I began to drive slowly allowing my passengers and me to look from side to side for the shop.

Suddenly, I looked up to notice that I was moving slowly but surely through a red light. And just as noticeable was the police car on the opposite side obediently waiting a change of the same light. "Oh no"! I informed aloud what some of the six already saw. I knew what would happen next. The police car did not disappoint that realization. When the light changed, their siren was sounded and their lights flashed a warning.

Pull over I did. I surrendered the registration and waited. The officer took a long time before returning to our car. I think he was a bit unsure of the registration that read Grey Nuns of the Sacred Heart. "Are you a nun?" he asked. I nodded my veil-less head in admission that "I am". Then, the unexpected! He removed his cap, handed me the registration and spoke words that should have comforted me: "I am not in the habit of giving nuns tickets."

We started out once more but the emotion of that event brought a blinding flood of tears causing me to pull up for an emotional cry. My passengers laughed. We returned back to our Motherhouse respite.

Fat girl's shop? Bathing suit? Yes, no? Faded in my memory!

How do we identify ourselves? How do others receive our response, even one that is true?

Remember when Jesus was arrested? There was a lot of activity going on as he stood before Pilate. Jesus had already been arrested and questioned in the Sanhedrin. He had already stood before Herod accused of blasphemy. Now before Pilate other voices would be heard.

Peter was there. The crowds had gathered. Surely the chief priests and leaders were there as well. But what was going on? Supposedly this Jesus had done something wrong. Was he the criminal some were claiming? Why were the leaders not influenced by his response that contained the truth? When they asked "Are you the Son of God?" he said "You say that I AM."

"I AM"! This is the name pronounced when Moses asked God his name.

Now, Jesus stood silent before Pilate and other voices were calling out, accusations were being made, punishment being suggested . . .

We can pause and hear the emotions of the moment—Pilate as he agrees with Herod finding no fault in Jesus, Peter as he denies knowing Jesus, the crowds calling out to crucify him and release Barabbas.

Not guilty? Jesus whom the leaders would not condemn received the punishment of the guilty. He wore his veil—a crown of thorns and his body striped in red from the beatings inflicted on him. Now he would go to that place called Calvary where he would release a thief and us from our guilt.

Not guilty! What about my adventure into Germantown? Oh I was guilty of breaking a traffic rule. But an officer of the law released me from punishment because of my response to his question: "You say that I am . . . a nun."

15

The Friendly 15

Ruth, Kathleen, Julia, Mary Elizabeth, Nancy (dubbed 8 or so) are the remaining group of the original 15. This was the group that gathered at the Motherhouse on what was called "entrance day". On that September day we would take on a group identity—postulants, a band. We didn't know each other but we each knew a Grey Nun and it was likely her inspiration that finally led each one here.

Postulants! Then, from this original group two received another identity—doyenne, the oldest and Benjamin, the youngest. Thus I became the first and a 17 year old the second. For what reason? No explanation was offered. But it was certainly the custom—a kind of anointing that harkened back to the sons of Jacob.

What really characterized this motley group of strangers was a sense of independence. It rose out of fifteen individuals who began to draw close despite the years between doyenne and Benjamin. That independence began to express itself when we anticipated what were to be—surprise events in our honor or holiday celebrations—by jumping the gun in planning them ourselves.

We found ways to befriend the professed sisters though casual contact outside of class was a no no. Somehow we initiated Sr. Pat—called it the peanut butter friendship oath. Our forbidden casual visiting was a warm experience slightly chilled by our meeting place—the walk in cooler. Other sisters made our forbidden list. I wonder now if any one of us admitted our "fault" or if these casual events remained in our Friendly bond.

"Friendly"! When were we first dubbed with that name? But we were that. We had our own meetings to discuss postulant life. I think we became groupie when we decided to perform—writing songs and gospels, dancing and putting on a play.

Had other groups ever presented themselves as we did, to the Mother General to entertain her? My episode of two broken legs further gathered us together as everyone found her role in assisting me over the healing weeks and over the rules of silence.

But dubbed we were and we lived up to that name by the concern we had for each other as well. When days came that this "band" was to experience the loss of a Friendly, one who chose to leave, the remaining Friendly found ways to say good bye despite the intended hush-hush departure of those days.

Before the end of our three year novitiate fifteen were ten. At our 25th jubilee six Friendly would emerge to celebrate.

Our days as the Friendly 15 carry fond memories of when we lived out this new experience called the postulant and novitiate years. Today, the spirit that engaged us for a season is now spread into communities where all that giftedness and sense of giving is realized, as we live blessed by the Holy Spirit. Now each has followed her call, our first call as baptized Christians, witnessing God's love wherever we can serve and be friendly to our neighbor and his needs.

Today we are fourteen—married, single and Grey Nuns aware of that first group relationship, now tucked in our memory wherever we are or whenever we meet.

Simon Peter, Andrew, James and John, Philip and Bartholomew, Thomas and Matthew, James, Thaddeus, Simon and Judas. This was the group that came together at Jesus' call. They gathered with him and they were identified as his disciples. The youngest among them, the Benjamin of the group was John. And Peter? While not named the oldest, he was the one who would be given the prime role—the Rock, the first pope. In the line of popes we might designate him doyenne.

Twelve followers. Disciples. They would suffer the loss of one among them but later name another to take his place. The twelve had walked with Jesus and received his commission to proclaim the kingdom of heaven "to the lost sheep of the house of Israel . . . to cure the sick, raise the dead, cleanse lepers, and drive out demons." I think of this walk, this time with Jesus as a "novitiate"—a preparation for their future walk, one guided by the Spirit.

After three years with the Master, who would have expected them to gather, as eleven disciples hiding in fear, disbelieving the event of his rising, waiting for the promise of the baptism with the Holy Spirit? What thoughts must they have shared as they waited? What memories held them together now?

It was Pentecost. In that place where they had gathered "there appeared to them tongues as of fire, which parted and came to rest on each of them. And they were all filled with the Holy Spirit." Peter, the one who had denied Jesus, stood with the Eleven and boldly proclaimed the certainty that Jesus was both Lord and Messiah.

Their identity as Apostles was ratified in that baptism. And, they would choose a replacement for Judas in order to remain twelve. We, the original Friendly, approached our profession day . . . with Spirit filled eagerness to be ratified as Grey Nuns. Later, still another would join the Apostles. Not among the official band of twelve, one called Paul would become a part of their role as "apostle".

They and we came away from our "novitiate" experience doing what Jesus had commissioned us to do—witness and serve. Like that group of twelve, fourteen of the original Friendly 15 have gone out into the world, to those places where God has invited our presence.

49
Modern What?

I was sitting on the edge of a bed in Buffalo when I was given the news—my assignment to teach in Queens. If my broken leg—newly plastered the day before ached, the words I heard sent a stronger ache into my emotional concern.

Modern what? Not again. I had just completed a teaching tour at our Academy located on the Motherhouse grounds. There I was surprised by the English curriculum—"modern English". The new approach required my after hours study—the challenge of morphemes, prefixes and affixes and the formation of words was followed by a bigger challenge—how to present the concept to a 7th grade class. A question lingered. Was this how I developed vocabulary and spelling in my school years? Lights out for us novices was 9 pm. I accomplished my study by creating a different and quiet lights out.

A new assignment and a new "modern". Modern math! When I cringed, having learned and excelled at traditional arithmetic, I was assured that the principal would meet with me each Tuesday evening after dinner and teach me this modern approach. I suppose that after dinner study was a bit better than my after hours experience.

Thus I entered the school on 49th Avenue with my broken leg and my broken knowledge of math and a bit of a crushed spirit. But I was soon lifted up by the accommodating efforts of my teacher-principal and of my 7th grade home room class.

Soon enough I became comfortable with both my new home and with life in the school. Forty five seventh graders greeted their new home room (and "modern math") teacher. They were especially happy about the change my broken leg brought about. The principal's first concern was my broken leg and using the stairs. She immediately changed the policy—now students would "change classes" rather than have teachers move class to class.

They were a good group of students and despite the 'math on my back' we experienced a successful teacher-student relationship. How thoughtful they were, these kids who were growing up in an ethnic neighborhood! From day one I was surprised by their kindness. Can you imagine a seventh grade boy coming to the convent and asking how he might help me in any of my duties there?! Yes, I did accept his help and our dining room never looked so clean!

My Tuesday sessions with the principal were faithfully executed—her teaching the teacher this new math. My early exposure to arithmetic emerged and faced the new. My arithmetic had required some memory—using the word "carry" in one's head as one progressed in a math problem. Now students "carried" but wrote down what we would have held in memory. Does that make sense?

Wednesdays followed. When a student had a question I had not yet been briefed on or understood, the smartest student was invited to the blackboard to demonstrate. Phew! This new math approach and a sharp student were apt to save me on many a Wednesday!

———————————

What was God the Father thinking when he decided to send his Son with a mission to become man? The job of creation, a great declaration of love and the assurance of His presence, was done. Yes, some angels had chosen to abscond from the original plan using their single choice—yes or no.

The creation of man in God's image was a great gift of Himself. The creature would take care of God's creation and even had the privilege of naming what God had created. Yet, man did not learn his lesson well. Is that what happened in those years when, for a time, English and arithmetic seemed to require a new approach? Were they not learning their lessons well?

God looked at what began in the beginning as good and now realized a need for a different approach, His "plan B". This plan emerged from the bosom of God, present from the beginning. It was expressed slowly with an invitation for his creation to meet the "I AM" and to accept His covenant, to accept their identity as God's chosen people.

They waited and in the fullness of time the "new man" came. He came with a modern message—with an updated version of relationship, of a New Covenant.

Jesus came with good news, came as teacher and invites us, the students, to the blackboard. Will we be like those smart students who, on any Wednesday, can demonstrate that we have learned the new approach?

66

Breaking In

One question people pose of us nuns is "when or how did you know you wanted to be a nun?" I can ramble around life events and offer an ultimately vague response. But I wish the question were something like: "how did you enter, get in the convent?" My answer would start with a humorous—"I broke in", referring to the fact that I actually entered with two broken legs.

Before that the way I "got in" was to make an application and take a psychological test. I did that but surrounding my responses was an event that closed the door for me. It was '66. A few years before that application, my sister in law died leaving an unhealthy husband and infant child.

A great ruckus arose over who would help my brother raise his new son. Strange how disagreement might lurk where love was at work! My parents became the caregivers in that atmosphere of stress. Even so, my mom responded to the uncertainty by an obsessive care of the baby. At the same time my brother continued to have health issues. Other tensions arose around that. And I chose to move from the household into an apartment. I needed the time away. But my concern remained with the family and I was very available to respond to the many needs that required my presence and assistance. We were all doing our best with the new baby and his father's un-diagnosed ill health.

But outside of our family home and my apartment, our story was not clear. That became evident when the ``Grey Nun letter came denying my entry into the congregation. It took another try. The sister, my professor and friend, who stood with me when I received the disappointing response reached out to me. She either knew or suspected the reason for my denial. Her suggestion was to tell the family story in terms of my response, my reasons for moving.

Praise God for the visit with the Superior General and her openness to the situation and my story. Another letter arrived. I "got in"—A Postulant in September 1967!

Surrounding that good news were two events—a bad slip on the ski slope and a slip on a cat's pee and into a desk. Both left me with hairline fractures. Both undiagnosed until I already "broke in" to the convent!

Who would expect another fall? Yes, another one while tripping onto the d'Youville College dorm roof where friends were gathering to view the sights of downtown and of the near by Peace Bridge. It would mean another cast, this time as I was making my first profession as a Grey Nun. Break number three!

This "breaking in" has been a series of painful experiences!

How did the first disciples "break" in? That is, how did they enter the company of Jesus? The stories are clear that he simply called the first twelve without any reservations or conditions . . . "Follow me".

One would think that they could not just pick up and leave family or jobs without some care before taking off with Jesus. After all Peter had a wife, his brother and others had fishing as their livelihood, their business. James and John had a mother. Matthew was a tax collector.

There was one who wanted to join Jesus. Remember his response when Jesus said, first, "sell what you have, give to the poor"?

Do we need to read into the scriptures and consider what the Twelve really had to do as they broke into this new life as disciples of Jesus? Was it painful for them to change their routines, their life styles, to become an itinerant with him who "had no where to lay his head"? Questions loom. What seems certain is that they were with Jesus for his three year ministry. We see them walking with him, praying with him, and as disciples we find them struggling with their Master's teachings.

This call to follow, to leave all behind, may or may not have been painful. Yet, as Jesus became a controversial figure, their experiences as his disciples were growing painful. After Jesus' death on the cross and his post resurrection appearances to them they would begin to take on their crosses.

When they were finally professed at Pentecost, these Apostles were filled with the Holy Spirit who would guide their lives but not keep them from the crosses they would endure.

We are called to follow. But painless? "Take up your Cross and Follow me"!

68

Our Muzzy

Have you seen the movie "Thoroughly Modern Millie"? Seeing it on TV the first time since the summer of '68 brought back a flood of memories from postulant days, when fifteen postulants were aspiring to be Grey Nuns.

One of the blessings of that first year encounter in the "nunnery" was a work vacation at an ocean beach home in Cape May. The work was that fourteen postulants headed to Cape May to our Grey Nun summer home. We arrived to open the beach house, to prepare it for professed sisters who both vacationed there and taught summer school at the house—on its porches, its parlor or dining rooms.

Being postulants meant that we were accompanied by a professed sister. She would oversee our work effort as well as our vacation play time. Our first response was that we could do this thing ourselves and did not need a professed overseer.

As it was, we quickly fell in love with the sister whom we would dub "Muzzy". Her first hint at not being a simple overseer was when she arranged for all of fifteen of us to see the movie, and at no cost . . . because she had a friend.

Muzzy was the name of the character of Carol Channing in the movie. What was common to movie Muzzy and our sister Muzzy was a deep husky voice. In the movie, Muzzy invited guests to her mansion beach home in Long Island. On the other hand sister Muzzy brought her guests (actually a work crew) to a beach home facing the ocean in Cape May.

Sister Muzzy really made our time there something more than all work. She, like movie counterpart Muzzy provided us with the gift of her personality and the model of a hostess and friend rather than the expected overseer we had imagined.

Yes, we had arrived with expectations about this week away. They were quickly changed when sister overseer showed her true face. We reveled in that transfiguration as our hostess opened the Cape May opportunities to her postulant guests—to the boardwalk, with trips for ice cream and the movies. She cut our work day so that after lunch we could enjoy swimming in the ocean. The beach house became a place where we prepared and enjoyed special dinners together and many evening get-togethers and party fun too.

When the week came to an end it was only fitting to honor our Muzzy with a surprise party marked by treats, with home made cards expressing our love, and tears for a new friend. Endings are often sad times when folks who grow close must separate for a time. We would return from the casual life at the beach house to the Motherhouse, to the halls where formality forbade conversation between postulants and professed sisters. When our week ended there remained winks and nods for our Muzzy when we recognized her in Sister Marcella in the halls of the Motherhouse

---

What expectations did Peter, James and John have when Jesus took them up the mountain to pray? Actually, they were overcome by sleep. Sounds like this wasn't going to be what they might have thought it to be. Oh, they knew Jesus, or thought they did. But drift away from this time with him?

What does this say about their response, their expectations to his invitation? We may have experienced similar responses when

Jesus called us to come away and pray. Difficult, perhaps to stay awake or to even pause and miss the real face of our host!

Like Jesus' guests on the mountain, we may become fully awake to see the face of Jesus . . . marked by a transfiguration, changed in appearance—able to see his glory. The apostles became frightened when a cloud cast a shadow over them. It was then that a voice spoke out and Jesus, their Muzzy, our Muzzy, was revealed—". . . chosen Son . . . listen to him".

At times, we may seem separated from, or not recognize, our Jesus-Muzzy but as the clouds pass we may pause long enough to listen to him . . . . or to give him a holy nod.

77
The Blizzard

The snow fell that day and blanketed Buffalo for a week. A call to my mother should have had the simple greeting—"Happy Birthday Mom". Today's greeting included—"Happy Snow Day!" Of course mom's birthday was one day and the blizzard celebrated a week.

My dad used to tell us about the mid '30s when snow covered Buffalo. Now it was 1977 and I heard President Carter proclaim Buffalo as a disaster site, and the mayor issue a no driving except for emergencies order. Work hours were restricted to a four day week and schools were closed.

This was different from the traditional Buffalo snow reputation which was usually over stated. A lake effect snow might last a day or two and then yield to a meltdown. Not so on January 28th.

On this January day of 1977, a group of us, nuns, found ourselves confined in our convent quarters. It seemed like we would experience the reverse of a common adage. "All work and no play . . ." was suddenly "All play and no work . . ." It was thus that we entered into a creative week.

All was new, nothing dull. We abandoned the car for a sled borrowed from a neighbor kid to go shopping. At each corner bags were removed from the sled and handed to a partner nun who had scaled the hill of snow and then returned bags back to the sled on the other side.

Each sister became a creator of a daily surprise dinner or specialty treat. I remember the kitchen counter being converted into our "local ice cream sundae bar", and with all the makings. Rosalie and I were partners in this reconstruction of the counter. We had spent the day preparing its conversion into a favorite ice cream parlor atmosphere. What a reward we experienced in the opening of our parlor when the line of sisters formed and each eagerly sought her favorite homemade sundae!

Episodes of "Roots" absorbed our interest. It was like a gift to all our Buffalo companions that the series ran through blizzard week.

A silly, improvised, racing car game engaged us age 35 to 85. Toy cars purchased at the local drug store were claimed by each and the races and a bit of penny gambling began.

We lived and laughed for a week. All play and no work does not a dull nun make!

They were just fisherman working their boats in the Sea of Galilee. Were they aware of the happenings at the River Jordan? That Jesus was baptized there by John, that the heavens were torn apart and the Spirit descended upon him, that he was called Son?

A storm was already brewing. John was arrested. Jesus was proclaiming the time of fulfillment and Jewish leaders were suspicious of this claim. In the midst of this, Jesus called two fishermen to follow him: "I will make you fishers of men."

A group finally formed around Jesus, leaving their nets, their work behind. Almost suddenly they began a new life experience—no longer fish but men.

Their days would be different from our blizzard week. When they were all in one place together, confined by fear, they would realize their mission to fish for men. Perhaps they were recalling how they walked with Jesus, challenged his parables, shared an unusual meal, learned about washing feet and welcoming the outsider.

Then the ultimate blizzard—a noise from the sky, a strong driving wind filled the entire house and not snow but tongues of fire blanketed each of them. They were no longer afraid but empowered for their commission to go out and fish for men.

During our "Blizzard of '77" the sisters at HAA Convent remained at home not afraid, but content to do our fishing mission through prayer and a bit of play!

1700

"Tipsy Nuns"

"You can't judge a book by its cover". So goes the old saying.

There was another "saying" that was birthed in the mid 1700s—les sours gris. It arose in the streets of Montreal when three women were walking to Mass one day. One, a widow and her two companions were holy women offering their days in works of charity and of compassion that was extended to Montreal's poor and most needy.

The widow Marguerite had devoted herself to the poor without neglect for the care of her two sons and the concern for clearing her late husband's debts and reputation. She had committed herself to the Father and his Providence even in the face of her experience of the Cross.

This is the content of the book, the story of the woman who extended her "Hands to the Needy".

But the cover? As the widow Marguerite walked along with her companions that day, she wore the traditional dress of the day—a widow's veil, a black cape over grey garment with a widow's black cincture hanging from around her waist. Her companions chose to wear the same color garb.

Most who know me have not seen me wearing that garb. It was known as a habit when worn in my day, the 1960s. It was the common dress—habit of our congregation, from the 1700s until around 1967. Today, sisters wear the dress of the day accompanied by a ring and cross to identify our unity with our founder. When someone asks why we are called Grey Nuns, I proudly reveal the legend—indeed the story.

That day when Marguerite and her companions walked along wearing grey, those who knew of her husband and his reputation for selling drink to the Indians, called out in derision: Les Sours Gris—in French Gris a double meaning—"grey or tipsy sisters". Marguerite accepted the slur as the name for her congregation.

We do not wear the traditional grey garb today but no matter what is our "cover" we are committed to compassionate love—the life story, the book, of Marguerite d'Youville.

The crown of thorns was pressed against his head. They covered him in a purple cloak. The message they connote was that he was a king or someone of royalty. The mockery, the double meaning in them hid the true story of Jesus.

One need only open the Bible to find the real meaning of Jesus' crown as king—the "I AM" of the revelation of God—king of the universe. Our faith recognizes the presence of Jesus, the Son, even in the act of creation.

Although he did not wear his crown or a regal robe when he entered Jerusalem, Jesus was welcomed with palms and hosannas. Did the people really know whom it was they were welcoming? Did they suspect that the man riding an ass was the long awaited Messiah, the Christ? Could they foresee Jesus lifted up on a cross labeled with his claim of kingship?? Or would they wonder that soldiers would gamble for the seamless white garment of a criminal?

The Jesus story is not wrapped in the signs of crowns or robes but unraveled in his everyday walk with his disciples. His was a commitment to the Father as his message of love, healing and forgiveness led him closer to the Cross.

To this day we are called to wear the cover of Jesus, of those first disciples. We're called by baptism to a challenge to witness to his story.

Our simple cover? We are called Christians.

1990
Project Flying Nun

Rome! The canonization of Marguerite d'Youville, our founder! My heart leapt at the possibility of being there. I had just started an adjunct position as associate professor of Spanish. Teaching would provide a salary above the stipend I received as a full time Campus Minister.

Twenty five interested sisters would be selected for the trip from a random drawing at the Motherhouse. I was not a winner. Others might travel if family or someone sponsored the trip. The big "but" was a response to my excitement. "But" one may not keep earned monies for personal use. All monies earned belong to the community. It is what poverty means in a religious congregation.

After I received the reminder, I shed some tears of disappointment and then dried them in the realization of my vow of poverty. When colleagues didn't understand and shared my disappointment, I had the opportunity to witness to the meaning of religious life and vowed living.

Shortly after, I received a phone call from Colonel Baker, Vice President of the Campus. He began, "I understand you have a problem." Yikes. Had he heard about my class behavior? About the incident in my Spanish class? It happened that a student was pushing me to my limit about her grade. In a moment of release, I tossed an eraser on the floor, an expression of my anger. Now, here was the VP, calling me to task??

No. Instead my tale of disappointment had reached his office via Robin a faculty member and Judy, president of the Campus Ministry Student Association. He wanted to assure me that they would start "Project Flying Nun" to raise the money . . . to send me flying to Rome!

And, what a project it was! Tickets were printed "Project Flying Nun" and Colonel Baker provided an under the counter TV for a raffle. The campus was alive with the enthusiasm of ticket sellers and buyers while I went on teaching my Spanish class.

Come December, I was a flying nun. In Rome I would be privy to the secrets of this city and the thrill of being present at the canonization of Marguerite as Saint.

––––––––––––––

What have I to say about this experience? As I pondered, I heard the Lord direct me to a channel and a program for a revelation, a now moment. And, voila! In that moment, out of the conversation going on about virtue, truth and freedom, I was drawn to the word "truth". Jesus wants me to share something here about truth, I thought.

So I found my way to the question posed by Pilate who asked Jesus: "What is truth?" His question to Jesus was the basic question for all of us. There is an irony in the scene where the question is posed because here, in front of the questioner, stands the Eternal Truth—Jesus himself, incarnate, human. His words proclaimed "I am the Way, the Truth and the Life. Peter recognized this in his admission: "Where else shall we go Lord, but to you? You alone have the words of eternal life."

Our answer to Pilate's profound question is that Jesus is the Truth. If it is truth that we seek, then it is to Jesus that we must come.

How often we need to pay attention to aspects of truth in the common activities of our life as well! My tear filled disappointment when I heard the truth—a reminder of my vow of poverty, encouraged me to recall the truth that I accepted years ago. It called me to the One who is the Way, the Truth and the Life. Each of us who makes a vow is called to express its truth by our lives—we become a witness to the Eternal Truth.

Was it in the acceptance of my vow that day in 1990 that Providence created another way to Rome? . . . and that I would be a "flying nun"?

1993

Circle the City with Love-

An experience of Philadelphia's poor.

We went into the City . . . to the neighborhood of 9th and Cambria, to circle the city with our love.

Sr. Eileen and I arrived in the City, and in the company of our guide, a social service sister, we walked through the neighborhood. Yes, we came to circle the City with our love. And, the City ignored us. There was no special welcome. Rather, it reached out and embraced us with the same ugly arms that had greeted its tenants that morning, the morning before and . . . Even the old parish on the corner closed its doors in 1993, overcome by neighborhood changes.

We were grasped by its arms of brick and concrete—row houses and streets—hot, sweating, without the comfort of trees stretching out cooling limbs to offer shade or to shadow the ugliness of squalor all about. They were arms like those with uncared-for leprosy—blistered, open with the insides pouring out, filthy, broken, a nauseating stench emanating from its sore spots. They were arms pocked by garbage—either bagged or "waiting", or strewn about, marking sidewalk and street with its own gross graffiti.

I felt too clean, a stranger in the midst of this embrace as I walked over bottle caps and broken glass and I moved aside in deference to broken furniture and trash in our path. As I peeled gum from my shoes, the thought of people being "stuck" here tugged at my heart.

115

Our guide seemed to sing the song to us as we tried to keep up with her rhythm, moving from street to street, door to door, person to person. She offered a loving heart to each person. We listened, we saw.

"Build bridges that unite", the song begins . . . . and we looked at them—people whose lives had known brokenness because of murder, rape, abuse, separation of family members, squalor, insecurity; people with names and faces and stories; people like Ruth, Delia, Gilberto . . .

"We are the hope for changing stones to bread" . . . more, we are confronted with the Gospel imperative of love—love that does not offer a stone when the need is bread. Yet, the stone-responses stand here where the need—the bread—is food,

Decent housing, sanitation of homes and streets, education (of rights and opportunities), physical and mental care!

Our guide's song is a living sound that circles the people of St. Bonaventure Parish. Her direct, vibrant, loving presence penetrates the tight grasp of oppression that binds this Hispanic community. When she goes out to meet her neighbors, this sister brings a deep concern for each person, a concern for the person's dignity and integrity unlike those political and social institutions that offer one sided help or those which neglect help completely.

What about our experience of a day with the poor? Sr. Eileen seemed drawn to return to a close bonding with the poor. To her gentle "Mucho gusto", her heart seemed to echo, "Hasta muy pronto". I suppose I am left listening to my heart and I know, even more now, that "Tuesday" assured me of presence "desde los ojos de los pobres".

For me I am left feeling that some of my prayer and response must be a litany once experienced in the street-chapel where the poor pray.

Our experience was a deeply spiritual walk. It was as if we put on the shoes of our founder Marguerite d'Youville or the sandals of Jesus for a little while . . . as observers Together they lifted up those in need, embraced them in their poverty whether it might be an abandoned baby or an enemy soldier, a Samaritan woman or a man born blind.

To those who did not have the experience of our Tuesday with the poor, to those who have not spent time with the materially poor, and yes, even we who took the walk, may take renewed inspiration as we read the gospels of Marguerite and Jesus.

Named "Mother of Universal Charity", Marguerite's compassion is recorded in Hands to the Needy"*. And, we need only open the Christian Gospels, especially Luke's stories, to discover the works of Jesus as he went about responding to the needs of the poor . . . even in his experiences of his "sabbaths with the poor".

8791

Silly Questions

My dear friend and sister, Marie Christine, loved to perform her rendition of a ditty called "Silly Questions". She drew this sing song poem out of her bag of jokes at many of our community gatherings. If it had been repeated x number of times, it was either because we enjoyed it or because we were willing to give her a platform to perform on. From my own bag, I am frequently asked to repeat "Why Fire Engines are Red".

But there was a day, in a convent on 8791S. Main St., that someone asked a silly question. Rather, it was more the silly answer that I remember.

The convent was attached to the far end of the elementary school. As the principal, I had reminded teachers that the convent was not equipped or insured to serve as a classroom. But teachers being teachers, it happened that one, a nun at that, chose to take a small group to the convent for a special class. That indiscretion would have passed unnoticed except that . . .

Later in the day, the teacher made a casual comment that while there the phone rang. She disregarded the message—a bomb threat—as some kind of joke. I immediately called the police. They chose to interview the sister. "How long were you in the convent", they asked. Not such a silly question at all I suppose! But the sister, now anxious in this confrontation with the law, began to count—"novitiate, junior professed, years teaching . . ." to establish just how long she had been a sister . . . been "in the convent".

There it was a silly answer! It was born in a moment of confusion, perhaps a bit of disobedience and guilt and certainly in response to a cop's question. For me it is a story to tell and re-tell and to laugh about. I am not sure the sister who stumbled over the count of years she had spent as a nun has kept the story as alive as have I. And if she hears it repeated along the way, I hope she enjoys the humor that could be found even in a very serious situation.

Oh, the kids enjoyed an early dismissal that day and the convent never blew up!

I reflected on what might be a silly question or a silly answer among some characters in scripture. What responses were made to questions and which part of the conversations was "silly"? What are the effects of "silly"?

Zechariah challenged the angel who was offering him an answer to prayer—a son in his old age. His response was disbelief—"I am an old man and my wife is advanced in years". Best to believe in angel messages! That response to an angel might be looked on as silly since it made him speechless.

Mary's "How can this be" to the angel Gabriel was quickly followed by a yes—"Be it done to me according to your word" and what at first might have sounded like a silly offer was done to her.

Jesus tried to offer clear answers to the silly questions posed by the Jewish priests and his captors when they asked if he was the king of the Jews. How did they not recognize his response—"I told you that I AM"? I AM, the name offered Moses when he asked "Whom shall I say sent me?" It was the name that motivated the Israelites to know that God was One and with them.

Peter kept a distance, hidden among the crowd, when Jesus was being questioned. Three times he denied their challenge that he was with Jesus. Silly. silly, silly denials. The cock crowed! Peter wept!

What of the criminals hanging near Jesus? One asks—"Are you not the Messiah? Save yourself and us." The other rebukes him for his silly question. Then he asks Jesus to be remembered in his kingdom. No silliness here. Rather an "Amen", an assurance that he would be with him in Paradise.

Remember when the women came to the tomb. Did they think the angels' question was silly? "Why do you seek the living among the dead?" It seems not since they made no questions but in belief immediately sought to share the good news.

Do we make silly questions or offer silly responses as we travel our spiritual journey? How easy to slip into the silly mode when people, confusion, confrontations, misunderstandings or fear engage us. Like the sister—or Zechariah or Mary or the accusers or Peter or the criminals or the women—all involved in the moment of the questions, we too may respond in an unexpected way. How silly of us!

"Kids" will be kids . . .

in each of us and at any age.

Within three days his Resurrection would proclaim—"gotcha".

The Golden Windows
by Laura E. Richards (1850-1943)
is about a boy who,
at the end of most working days,
would sit on top of a hill
and look at a far-away house
that appeared to have golden windows.
As he did so he wished that one day
he could live in a wonderful house like this.
One day he sets out to find the house
and learns an important lesson about life.

1952

. . . Without Marilyn

45

After Hours

A float is a large flat vehicle pulled by a truck cab and carrying an exhibit. For college students preparing for Moving up Day, our task was to transform that flatbed into an exhibit of class pride. Our tools were our hands. Our materials were an assortment of paper much of it a kind of Kleenex. Our plan was the mix of ideas offered by our creative student efforts.

The whole project began with the tedious task of making roses. That task was an after full days of classes and homework job. With it came a bit of finagling. It required pulling the wool over the eyes of nun monitors and house mothers.

The plan emerged out of the minds of these grown up kids. We would meet late that night in the d'Youville "coffee shop". Well, in the 60s that room was really a kind of cafeteria and gathering room between classes. It was housed in the lower level of the building on 320 Porter but also had a side door to the outside. Residents lived on the fourth floor and under the eye of a sister. Other residents lived in a house at 45 Richmond, a few blocks away, under the eye of a house mother. Then there were the day hops.

Now it was important to bring all the elements together after hours to begin making the hundreds of roses required for our exhibit. This without disturbing either the sleeping nun at "320" or the house mother at "45"!

Step one. Fourth floor residents sneak down quietly to open the outside door of the coffee shop. Step two. Day hops arrive at the resident house at a prescribed time to pick up those who also sneaked out quietly. Step three. We arrive and are admitted to the coffee shop. Step four. We spend an almost all nighter creating the tissue paper roses. Step five. Reverse steps four to one and get a couple hours sleep. Repeat all steps another day!

In the end our roses were part of the exhibit that transformed the flatbed into a float. Each class float would pass the front of the college where students and nuns gathered to cheer their particular efforts before the parade around the neighborhood. Hours and hours of creative work were on display for onlookers.

Now, I wonder. Did those nuns and housemothers even pause to reflect on how busy college students accomplished this major transformation? Or did each have an eye open and chuckle at all the sneaking about?

Jesus was known to go away to pray. It is likely that most prayer times were at night, after hours so to speak. Worn by travel or after days busied by meeting the needs of those who pressed him during the day, Jesus would slip away to be alone.

There was an occasion when he called Peter, James and John to accompany him. They went off with him to Mt. Tabor. It must have been evening since the three were "overcome by sleep". They awoke and saw Jesus in his glory. He was transfigured before them.

The Bible never gives any physical description of Christ. The closest thing we get to a description is in Isaiah 53:2, "He had no beauty or majesty to attract us to Him, nothing in His appearance that we should desire Him." Among his apostles, Jesus apparently didn't stand out as physically different. Even Judas had to identify him with a kiss because Jesus blended in.

Yet here before them Jesus appeared shining, a dazzling brightness emanated from his whole Body and his garments were white as snow. Here, after hours a change, a manifestation occurred offering the three a foretaste of glory and the assuring voice of God, "This is my chosen Son; listen to him."

Scripture tells us that they told no one about what had happened there, on the Mount . . . after hours.

60

Rubber Bands and a Green Slip!

School 60! A once bubbling building of academic activity now stands boarded up, bearing the stigma of old age, empty of all life. It's as though it is hiding the memories of other generations, of kids who walked to this place and created the life within. Now it stands there, lifeless and warning a new generation to stay out.

As I drive past the Ontario Street structure, I pause and remember. I am part of that generation, one that lifed the school. How different we were as kids—even misbehaving kids, from kids of today.

Misbehaving! For us there was a certain innocence even about the bad things we did. There were no weapons, no physical assaults on teachers, no killings or bomb threats . . .

But there was one assault that comes to mind. It involved rubber bands. We were in the required music class. Our task was to sing or to learn to sing. Our teacher was a small, frail woman whom we were sure wore a curly black wig. Now why did the department of education ever provide seventh graders with a teacher that was someone we would poke fun at? We became out of her control when the rubber bands began striking out. I don't think they were aimed at her but rather it was a kind of fun battle, guys against guys mostly but maybe some gals as well. And certainly the disruption was against music class! I didn't have my own supply of the weapons but I did pick up a rubber band from the floor and try to enter the fracas. Didn't work! I had no previous training!

The upshot of this activity was that the entire class was sent to a special room there to await an individual meeting with the principal, Mr. Hempstreet. When my turn came I pleaded not guilty and as evidence I would prove I did not know how to load and shoot. As luck would have it the rubber band seemed to take on a life of its own hitting the principal smack on his face. Guilty! Was there a punishment? What I remember is that he dubbed me "Ruth couldn't shoot the rubber band Penksa".

Then, there was the green slip incident. It was not an assault just a provocation, a way to annoy another one of those teachers of special classes. It was the sewing class and the teacher was a laughable character to us. The assignment was to bring in material for making a slip. I deliberately chose a bright green heavy cotton material. All the girls laughed at my choice but the teacher's calm topped my effort to ridicule the assignment. I came home with a green slip.

Rather, it was Marilyn, with her roll call response: "ugha boo, ugha ugha boo" that made us roll with laughter as the best of misbehaving that day, in that sewing class, with that stoic Miss G.

In the midst of the Roman Empire there stood a structure that housed the Law of Moses—the Ten Commandments—Judaism. The Jews had been a people—God's people for generations, a people who guarded this edifice religiously. As they awaited the coming of a Messiah something was stirring among them. A new structure was rising!

Paul, a Jew, was there. Paul covered his Jewishness with the armor of a Roman soldier. He took on his role as a soldier, persecuting that emerging new movement of renegade Jews who seemed a threat to Rome.

But how did he look on his fellow Jews who were members of this new movement? How did he judge their behavior, their new faith?

This was a new generation of Jews. They were being dubbed "Christians", followers of the Christ. They were leaving the old structure that had bound them together for generations before. Had Paul heard about Peter's commission by Jesus to "build my Church"? What would that mean to Paul—Jew, soldier and citizen of Rome? How did he judge this movement? A new structure was rising! It was inviting even the gentiles. Were the Jews who entered misbehaving?

It was precisely as Paul was going about "rubber banding" those Christians that he was confronted by the "Principal". Paul was called to task, questioned about his actions by the Spirit that overtook him and the words spoken aloud: "Paul, why are you persecuting me?" For Paul, it became time to put aside what had been a task for him and to set out in other directions.

Looking back at those days in School 60, was our misbehavior a kind of persecution? Were our rubber bands aimed against those who took us away from the traditional readin', writin', 'rithmatic and tried to expand our world, set us out in other directions and possibilities?

I am not a good singer and I certainly don't sew (or make slips). But like Paul, I've heard a voice urging me on to other possibilities . . . you may have heard that voice too.

62

"john" Tales

What is the fascination that students have with bathrooms when playing tricks, when misbehaving? Sometimes they are clever and the culprits escape leaving the results of their adventure in the cold case files of the principal. At other times, the young guilty tricksters offer a reason for their junior felony that requires a hidden laugh on the face of the investigating principal. It may only be an inquisition by second graders about the structure of the boys' bathroom. The truth be told these misbehaviors are committed even when we are looking!

I think of the case of missing door locks in the girls' john—the cultural jargon for "bathroom", at Melrose.High. The result was that the lock of each stall had been removed. The questions loomed: How was this possible during the school day? Where were the teacher mentors? What tools or ingenuity was used? Who were the girls involved? Where were the missing locks? As I remember the answers escaped the true revelation even before the best investigator-principal ever, "Sr. Mary Investigator". No punishment, just the purchase and replacement of new locks. Thus the intricacies involved in the event remain in my cold case memory about "locks" in a small private high school in southeast Pa . . . .

Years later, miles away on rte. 62 in western New York there was another small private school along a stretch that produced more than corn—ICS elementary school.

During my tenure as principal there I now had the role, among others, of chief investigator of kid crimes. One such misbehavior

133

was the case of wads of wet toilet paper appearing on the walls and ceilings of the boys' john. I never caught the one or ones involved. The punishment was imposed on all bathroom users—report to me before and after each john visit to verify the condition of the room.

I was a new principal and some second grade boys surrounded me to ask important questions. Perhaps the former principal hadn't satisfied their curiosity. The question of the day: "Why do the girls' stalls have doors and the boys' stalls don't?" I answered with my own questions: "How do you know they don't?" and "Why does that bother you?". To the first they admitted that the girls told them. To the second, one little guy replied: "You sit down to take a "c—p" and everyone can see you." Urging him to use better language I asked "Don't you know another word to use?" Out of the mouths of babes came "Yes, but you sure don't want to hear it!"

No changes followed the inquiry—boys' john stalls remained without doors!

I think of those situations: the lock abusers who were silent somewhere among their fellow students but whose actions were evident; the boys with concerns who shouted their opposition to try to get their way. Their inquisitors were principals faced with the need to make decisions.

I think of the arrest of Jesus. What did the crowd and conspirators among them want to hear as Jesus stood before them and Pilate, his inquisitor? And, what of Pilate who was confronted with making a decision?

Did they want to hear what was really on Pilate's mind—that he thought Jesus was not guilty of the charges laid on him? Or that

Pilate was thinking of his wife's dream calling Jesus "righteous? Or that he feared his own political position as governor?

The crowds persuaded by the chief priests were persistent. They knew what they wanted and how they would respond. There was one word on their minds—"Crucify!" They knew the way to accomplish this was to give Pilate another option—one that they wanted and that Pilate might justify! Jesus or Barabbas? "Barabbas" was the word shouted out by the crowds! Pilate yielded. But as he washed his hands he was saying "I am innocent of this man's blood." Crucifixion followed this unholy inquiry!

Each of us—principal, governor or parent, teacher, friend—may find ourselves facing the actions or demands of others that require our response, our judgment. We are called to weigh them carefully, compassionately, yet guided by principles.

When is the time, if any, to simply wash our hands?

63

"Gotcha!"

I love teaching boys! Oh, girls are really ok too. In fact, I had just finished my first year of teaching at a local girls' Catholic High School. But, there is something different about a class of boys. It was '63 and Hutch Tech High in Buffalo offered me such an experience.

The school provided an excellent education joining technical hands-on studies with required academic background for specific fields such as engineering. Clearly, students were prepared both for a profession and readiness to enter college.

The boys were required to wear a uniform—slacks and blazer or sweater and of course a tie. Should the tie be accidentally left at home, one was available for twenty five cents in the counselor's office. It was a lot easier to deal with attitude about this "tie" requirement than with the girls' attitude over banned bouffant hair styles or skirt lengths.

Antics! I think they are more a boy thing. They are "gotcha" moments. Some are thoughtful and vivid responses although rather unconventtional. Others, well they are those more prankish efforts that require a bit more of an investigative approach by the teacher.

I taught Spanish but rounded out my hours with one class called Economic World. When the topic of capitalism was being covered, I apparently suggested that it was like Campbell's tomato soup with multiple necessary ingredients, not just tomatoes. The suggestion must have been made not just once but whenever I spoke that word—capitalism. One such time (ever to be the last), the description was spoken and there occurred an immediate response from a class of thirty sophomore boys. Without a blink my desk was topped with thirty cans of Campbell's tomato soup . . . their "gotcha!" moment.

A beautiful red apple appeared on my desk. I picked it up to discover the back had already been eaten and the mystery gift giver had not waited for a thank you. Study hall with fifty students provided its own challenges. It required that my eyes had to scan the room frequently to maintain a study atmosphere. There was a student whom I had reprimanded for his lack of work ethic. In response, he began to bring a newspaper to read during the period. I was duly impressed until I discovered he was keeping his eyes on me . . . through two tiny holes in the paper. Likely he was thinking "Gotcha!"

"Win over the behavior of a student by seeking his confidence with a task". The words, or something like them, came as reminders to a second year teacher from a Psychology of Education class. I took the paper peeper aside and told him in confidence that there were some dirty words on a desk. Would he come in some time and clean the desk for me? The next day when I arrived for the study hall, there he was noisily scraping away at the desk top. My whispered "What are you doing?" prompted his loud, public, "Well you asked me to get rid of the dirty words." Laughter from the forty nine others filled the study hall that day.

The school was taking a collection for a charity event and each homeroom was asked to contribute. A prize would be offered for the highest donation collected. Combining my Spanish and artistic talents, I made a matador and a bull. Using a chair and desk, I climbed up to a precarious height and placed them against the wall above the blackboard, one at each end. The object—as we moved toward our goal, the matador and bull would be moved closer to each other. One observant student, perhaps an artist himself, approached to notify me, "The bull is a male". Wondering just what he meant, I investigated. My bull was now anatomically complete having been mysteriously reached by an artistic, biological, climbing student . . . and I never saw it happen. A real "gotcha!"

It seems that Jesus could do no good. His accusers cited the serious misbehaviors, the litany of his faults: healing on the Sabbath, claiming to be the Messiah . . . a king, opposing payment of taxes, disrupting activities at the Temple, misleading the people . . .

The overall "antics" of Jesus were outside the tradition of his Jewish heritage and the Law. They were behaviors that disturbed the many who listened, the teachers and clerics as well as the Roman leaders, Pilate and Herod. However, in a time and place—in the fullness of time, Jesus had come, not to change the Law but to fulfill it. His actions and his words were being disregarded and often he presented them in parables to "announce what has lain hidden".

Not guilty said Pilate Not guilty said Herod. Guilty cried the crowd. Thus, in the tradition of releasing a prisoner, Barabbas was freed and Jesus' sentence became death. Within three days his Resurrection would proclaim—"gotcha".

As a teacher, I look on the teen age behavior as an expression peculiar to their time and place . . . as their parables. We "read" them, break them open and try to understand their stories. Classroom laws were broken. Guilty?

Years later, in another time and place, there is a sound of accomplishment proclaimed in their adult life, once laid hidden in teen age students, now echoing: "gotcha".

80

Our Own Table

We were sitting around a table in our favorite coffee café. Somehow the Sunday stop after Mass had become a ritual for four. As I glanced around at our gathered group on this Sunday I realized that we had grown both in age and number. One boasted that she was 80 when someone guessed her in her 60s. Others offered being in their 50s, 60s 70s. And, on any Sunday, as on this one, the number at table might be increased requiring extra chairs that squeezed us in shoulder to shoulder.

Joe was the first to join the club of four as a regular. Actually, we had intruded on his space when a table was not available. What a guy! A burly fellow and designing engineer by profession he shared our faith and our conversation. Other regulars from our parish were likely to join us—like Ron, retired cop and choir member and his wife Gail a retired social worker. And do you believe that there was another common sharing when Joe, Ron and Gail realized they had common friends!

We were at "our" table but often conversations spilled over to others near us and often conversations revealed common friends or experiences. It was almost as though the table had just grown longer.

In this atmosphere I remembered when we were kids. At family dinners like Thanksgiving or Christmas there were separate tables—one relegated for kids and one for grown-ups. At the small kids' table we were separated from the conversation going on at the adults' table. I can picture the scenes but cannot now hear the chatter at our kids' table. Do you remember this kind of seating arrangement as a kid? How did you feel about it?

I think separate tables had its advantages—lacking adult scrutiny on our every move. When we ever did join the grown-up table it seemed that a one sided conversation prevailed: Look what you did! Don't pick at your vegetables! Use your napkin! No you can't leave until you clean your plate! Drink your milk! Oh, another spill!

Our kid table had allowed us the freedom of behavior and chatter despite our kid mishaps. Somehow today as we gathered at our coffee café table we grown ups were like kids not bound by the old adult rules. Rather we chuckled about the sugar on one's lips and all helped clean up another's coffee spill . . . with no echo of a past "look what you did!"

Were all the men seated at the Passover table grown-ups? adults? Twelve had gathered and were seated at Jesus' table, Jesus the itinerant preacher. Among the gathered were John, the youngest, and the burly Peter, married and a fisherman. Several others were fisherman as well; one may have had noble blood, another was a zealot (in politics of anarchy), one a wealthy tax collector and one with a bad reputation.

What conversation might be heard as Jesus spoke to the motley group at table with him? Jesus began with words that they must repeat over simple bread and wine—"Do this in memory of me". Then in an unexpected action he knelt, and after washing their feet—"so you also should wash one another's feet". The words spoken, the actions, would change their ways forever:" But there must have been a kid among those at this table—who ate and whose feet he washed—because Jesus next spoke firmly: "And you are clean, though not every one of you."

Judas left the table to participate in a betrayal priced at 30 pieces of silver. Just who was this Judas "kid"? Seated among the twelve he seems to be out of place with the words and actions of Jesus—perhaps still infested by a life of misdeeds. So he does go from there to follow through with his malice. But he changes his mind . . . a kid's wavering decision. Perhaps he sees for the first time what 30 pieces of silver mean to the Romans and to Jesus. In guilt he, chosen by Jesus to be an apostle, now he responds by overlooking Jesus' words of love and forgiveness spoken when they had first walked together.

Was Judas seated at the wrong table? Had there been a kid's table would things have been different?

99

When One of Those Bottles Happens to Fall...

. . . ninety nine bottles of beer on the wall! The suggestion is that one had been drunk leaving those 99. Well, on this class bus trip to the Poconos the beverage of choice was not beer and it seemed that more than one bottle was tested en route!

The freshman and sophomore classes were headed to the Poconos for a day trip at a site that offered a variety of outdoor activities and that one unexpected activity. Two nuns, a lay faculty member and a mother were the overseers of this day of adventure. Our task—just watch for the welfare of the playful students that none would get hurt.

On arrival, rooms were assigned in groups of four allowing the girls a place to change clothes for appropriate activities. Soon we were in the dining room eager for a lunch and the beginning of a full day. It was then that the one unexpected activity began to rear its head. A few girls left the table, apparently not feeling well and blaming the pickles they had nibbled on during the trip.

After an overseer huddle it was determined that the girls were ill after consuming "something", other than pickles, during the bus ride. We wanted an answer without acknowledging our suspicion or questioning the girls. Our tactic was to find the evidence but not invade their privacy. Well, not entirely. We entered a room, and eyes closed slipped a hand into suitcases and felt around. If we happened to touch a "bottle" in the bag, we took note of the owner's name and left the evidence behind.

Then we were caught in the act by a student who returned to her room. She was the most innocent student in the class! On our order, "Leave!" she did. Did she tell others what she saw? If so, we wondered how the girls enjoyed the day knowing what we knew and what we did not reveal to them about the discovery.

A phone call to the principal directed us to remain silent, to tell no one, that she would deal with the issue when we returned that evening. And deal with it she did. In the way that only our "judge" would—she "held court" at ten that night. "I will interrogate them", she insisted, and one by one the culprits faced their judge. Punishment fell on the entire two classes—no class trip next year. I don't remember if she actually carried out the sentence.

When we read about Jesus and his healing of the deaf, the dumb, the blind, the leper it is good to reflect on just what is going on. It is easy to center on the outcome—someone is healed. The outcome of the class trip was that the class was punished. But interesting to both is the actions of those involved leading up to the outcome.

Like the principal who ordered us to "tell no one", that was something that Jesus did on several occasions. There was the leper who asked to be made clean, the man deaf and with a speech impediment who begged for healing, the blind man who asked "that I may see". Each was told to "tell no one". But did the observers, the Joannes in the crowd, honor that admonition when they saw the outcome? Did those healed, or any possible onlookers, actually remain silent?

The principal chose to take the girls aside and interrogate each alone. I found it interesting that Jesus chose to take the deaf man away from the crowd and the blind man away from the village to heal them. They already had asked Jesus to heal them. Was there a reason, a need, for Jesus to ask again what they were seeking . . . and in private? After all, at other times scripture reveals Jesus in the act of healing, responding in the midst of the crowds.

Alone or in the midst of a crowd, whether they told or remained silent, one thing is certain. Jesus continued to go about healing.

127

A Run Away Kid

A stark, bright ray of light awakened me from dreamless sleep as I lay huddled on a park bench. I unwrapped my only cover, the fetal-body warmth that had warded off the damp night air. Then came a voice belonging to the figure that gradually took shape as my eyes accepted the light and my surroundings. It was a cop! "What are you doing here?"

When you are thirteen years old and running away from home, all you need is a policeman to interrupt your journey! After a brief interrogation, I was returned, bike and run-away bundle, to an anxious mom where the door and a heart was always open at this place—127 Riverside.

Quo Vadis? Where was I going? After a typical mom-kid argument, I had packed a few necessities and took off on my recent acquisition, a thirteen dollar bike. Destination—Aunt Frances' home where I was sure to be comforted in my tribulation and assured that I was a mistreated and misunderstood child. And, definitely, I had made the right decision to run away.

Aunt Frances, my mom's sister, was also my God-mother. She lived about fifteen miles from us. I had made the trip by bike frequently under better circumstances. Often I made the trip there after school and returned after breakfast the next morning in time for school. I think it may have taken about two hours each way.

On this occasion, however, I started out but was greeted by an unexpected weather condition—strong wind. I had peddled against its strength for several minutes when I realized that today was not a good afternoon for this particular escape to Aunt Frances'. Since my trek had ended very near the park, also just a few minutes from home, I went there and took refuge on a park bench to ponder my situation and re-strategize. In the midst of my planning I found respite on the uncomfortable bench. Evening and sleep fell upon the unaware run away. It was here that I was discovered and the direction I was headed now led to home.

When I think back of childhood days and mom-daughter relationships, what strikes me is the unconditional love of a parent for a child. How does a mom or a dad, continue to love an unruly off-spring; to forgive before a penitential word is spoken?

Day to day peer relationships aren't like that. On the job relationships aren't based on that kind of love. Even sibling ties come unloosed under stressful situations. The world community fails daily as it measures relationships by getting even.

But, there is the mom who welcomes home her prodigal daughter. Her loving response echoes the parable: "We are going to have a feast, a celebration."

I wonder why the younger son in Luke's parable really took off. What lured him away from the comfort of a parent who obviously loved him so deeply? How far can a daughter or a son run away from home and love? A more illusive question for me is "how could the father be so welcoming, hold the child in his heart as though nothing had ever changed his love for the one called prodigal?"

My mom, and yours, are called the first teachers. They are the imitation of the God whose language of love is burned into their hearts, whose flames are indistinguishable. Like the father in the parable, my mom always gifted me when there was a hint of separation in our relationship. No "so you're back, huh!" Rather, I was wrapped in her warm embrace. She would quickly go the store and return with a gift for me, a blouse or sweater. Did I need a cup of hot chocolate? The welcome, the gift, the drink—all symbols of a deep and abiding, unconditional, celebrated love.

Perhaps Jesus told this parable not so much to remind us of the Father-God and the love he has for us but to let us know that we can experience that love between each other. It may be the key to the commandment that we honor our father and mother because they are the living truth of the existence of unconditional love.

168

War Games

What games do children play? I think that games speak of the culture of the day. Anyway, I was living on168 Germaine Street during World War II. This was still a time when kids played outside (only until dark) and spent time in the local playgrounds or making up games. TV had not yet made a popular debut. Creativity was required and the war provided ideas.

What I remember is being a third grader and having a whole army of soldiers made of metal. They reminded me of looking like chessmen. So, I would join with neighborhood kids and share my army. One side would be American, the other Nazi Germans.

We lived next door to Ramie, Ramie—short for Raymond. At times he was my play companion. There was plenty of space in our backyard and a back porch as well. One day we were playing "war". No not the card game. That would have been the better option-, slamming down a card and calling out "war". But that day, "our war" was just winding down. The Americans had won. I had won! Now the judgment was made on the Nazi German, Ramie.

Of course that meant punishment. What kind of punishment was inflicted on real war prisoners? Where did the idea of hanging come from? Is that what happened to Nazi prisoners? But hanging it was. To carry out the sentence, I placed a cord around my prisoner's neck. He stood at the top of the rail-less steps. I made the command that he jump. And jump he did. Not on to the next step but off the side.

Actually, I saved him (not very American of me). We were playing. He or I should have been more careful. I pulled his shirt collar over the red bruise and urged him, "Don't tell your mom." Now how does a young kid hide a bruised neck? Moms always insist on a bath or at least a warning to wash your dirty neck, that followed by a checkup.

The deed was done. Ramie went home. He squealed or his mom noticed the neck. No matter, her visit to my mom would now mean a small war between mom and daughter. And mom's win. They must be American!

Jesus grew up in an atmosphere of war. The Romans dominated an empire and imposed harsh punishment on those who were defiant of their rules and regulations. Soldiers were armed and present daily among the people. Their enemy was often the poor and any unarmed who would even speak against Roman authority.

The Jewish leaders were another kind of warrior. Their arms against defiance were words and accusations and possible expulsion from the Temple. Jesus carried no arms. His army was twelve fishermen. He walked with them in the midst of these two factions as a peace maker, a healer. He wore sandals, a tunic and had no where to lay his head.

The Jewish and Roman leaders became suspicious of Jesus' behavior and his words. Interesting that they were really on opposite sides yet their attacks on Jesus converged.

In a time when the Jews were concerned about the coming of a Messiah, they closed their faith to the one who might be their "King". And the Romans feared that Jesus wanted to be their "king". Neither description of Jesus seemed to define the man whom they feared would be the "king". After all, what Messiah would be so poor, so un-kingly? What King would present himself to overthrow Rome with a small unarmed army?

Yet, Jesus became the target—the Jews and the Roman leaders won an undisputed war. There was a judgment and a punishment—hanging. Nails tore into his already scourged flesh as he was lifted up on a cross. The deed was done.

At the foot of the cross a mother stood weeping. How she must have wanted to hold him close, to bathe his bruised body! Did her thoughts go back to a manger, her new born babe wrapped in swaddling, and to songs and gifts offered to a "King"? Was there a "yes" in her heart now? The war game was over and a Jewish mom had surrendered her Son.

1952
A Kid Without Marilyn

My eighth grade classmates called me forth. Even before I could claim any oratorical charism, they urged me: "Join the speaking contest. You'll be good!" Thus began an interesting journey that would forge a trail from a first trial and failure to another trial and . . .

The essay I chose was, "The House with the Golden Windows." My prompter was Marilyn, a favorite and intelligent classmate. Her task: whisper the next word or phrase should I forget. The rule was that Mr. B, our teacher, would stand up to signal that a speaker had a minute left to complete her presentation.

As I stood before the school assembly, the words of the essay flowed from the mouth of the young teen who was favored to win this contest. Then the unspeakable happened. I stopped. No words followed. Marilyn, totally engrossed in listening, failed to follow the text. I was alone. In sympathy for the speechless orator, Mr. B. stood up before the appointed time allowing me to leave the stage.

Yes, I left that stage. But a new challenge became a stage for me. I recognized that the embarrassment of that event was less a concern than the fear of public speaking itself. What could I do? High School provided oratorical opportunities. There was the debate class where we practiced the art of argumentation and the drama course with an emphasis on developing one's interpretive and expressive skills. Each was a valuable moment on my stage and I enjoyed walking across it in the security of four walls and twenty five companions . . . Each class reached into a part of me, embraced and nurtured gifts yet unexpressed. Still that unspoken fear lingered.

Oh no! Spoken words stirred up the memory of words unspoken on a stage four years earlier: "our drama class of seniors will be putting on a Christmas play" . . . in public! . . . during the school assembly!" As the teacher assigned the parts, my downcast eyes and tightened body were rejecting the possibility of my being chosen. I breathed in relief as the last person was selected. The next words turned it all tipsy turvey. And, Ruth, you will do a presentation of "Keeping Christmas" by Henry Van Dyke.

Alone, I would be alone in front of the assembly. No actors to surround me. No classmates at my side. Quick flashes of the past renewed my fear. However, this was the present—1952. There was no Marilyn, no Mr. B. to get me off the stage. Instead, there was Miss Zeh to get me on stage, encouraging me with the wisdom of the ages, "Do the thing you fear and the death of fear is certain." Oh, I trembled as I waited my turn that day. But when I left the stage it was after I spoke the last line: ". . . and, if you can keep it for a day, why not always?"

Today as I look back, I remember that line of the piece by Van Dyke but not another word of it or of "The House with the Golden Windows. Today, at an older age, where is a Marilyn offering a whisper when a now grown kid needs her?

Isn't it interesting to look back at some stage of our life and to see it in view of who we are today? A poet once said, "All life is a stage and we are the players."

We are the players . . . chosen, called by God, called by name even before we experienced the warmth of a mother's womb, the light of birth, or our first steps . . . onto our personal stage.

Chosen, for particular roles, to share particular gifts, so that the play is a success.

Some might label this predestination. I like to believe that God shared a piece of himself—a free will, a will to choose good. That is what we bring to the stage of our life. That is our most precious gift. As we put on our identity and play our part we do so by interpreting the role, freely, but directed by God's grace. Yet, we sometimes falter.

Peter heard the words, words in our hearing as well: Before the cock crows you will deny me three times". Peter stepped onto a special stage in his life. He heard the Lord call his name: "You are Rock". Yet as he put on this graced identity, and even knowing Whom it was that called him, Peter yielded to fear and failed three times. Like Peter, there are times when we fall silent, when we fail in our parts. It's then that we need to heed the Prompter's whisper.

The Truth Be Told...

but all in good time

ne'er another Messiah... only the taste of His Body and Blood!

Joyce Murphy of Kenmore lends her voice for the enjoyment of some of her own neighbors. She has been a volunteer for about five years.

"I'm a voice person," Murphy said. "I sing and try to do things that are voice connected."

Murphy learned of the need for volunteers in an article on the Radio Reading Service. Now she volunteers once a week for an hour and a half reading articles, many from The Bee papers, on tape. And she is willing to read more if Sikorski is in a pinch because her job at the Fire Academy in Cheektowaga is close to the service.

"It's so convenient. I'm surprised I didn't start doing it sooner," she said. "I love that it helps other people."

a helping voice

Joyce Murphy of Kenmore volunteers her "voice" for the Niagara Frontier Radio Reading Service in Cheektowaga which broadcast daily readings of newspapers, magazines and other publications for print-handicapped people.

2

Behind the Curtain

I am a proud. member of the d'YC Class of '62. My memories of my d'Youville College days are mixed with the work required for classes, the enthusiasm for and participation in activities, the need to earn the tuition with after class jobs, and the turmoil surrounding illness, new life and death in my family.

One has to work at balancing those life demanding challenges. They do not happen in a clear order or list that one can check off when completed. It is a play and we are the actors stepping forward when our lines draw us from behind a curtain.

There was a time when I stood on the d'YC stage, in front of the college audience. And yes, in front of the curtain. It seems we were promoting an event—perhaps the traditional spring carnival. I was a sophomore in 1960 and the coordinator of the event. What I don't understand was how I was coerced to participate in the skit except that my classmates were aware of my talent . . . or, rather, lack of it. I was not a singer, having been informed by my dad that I sang off key. In that case, why me mouthing a song with Loretta, the class soprano, providing words from behind the curtain?

The masters of performance, the devious team that prepared the skit had something up their sleeves—comedy. I suppose it would be funny for me to mouth the song if the audience knew it was not my voice and very likely they would.

But the hilarity, the laughter in response to my effort was unexpected and—as the saying goes—bringing down the rafters. I was not fully aware of the intended comedy. The audience was gifted to experience it in its fullness when Loretta revealed herself—peeking out from behind the curtain and the one in front becoming the object of an unexpected comedic scheme. We had started out as two students in on the secret but somewhere only one became privy to the scheme.

I suppose that is akin to our lives when balancing takes an unexpected turn and the best laid plans reveal what was hidden behind a curtain.

We remember how the chief priests and elders schemed to testify against Jesus, accusing him of blasphemy, persuading the crowds against him. Jesus stood mute on his stage. He refused to answer the charges and even Pilate was amazed by his silence.

Because of that devious behavior Jesus was crucified. As he was mouthing a cry to God—"Why have you forsaken me?"—bystanders expected Elijah to appear. So they waited. Jesus cried out again in a loud voice and gave up his spirit.

Then, the unexpected! A truth peeked out from beyond the utterances of Jesus, from a sanctuary torn open. There was an earth quake and revelation—tombs were opened "and the bodies of many saints who had fallen asleep were raised."

Certainly the scheming priests and elders had not admitted the truth of who it was that hung from a cross on a stage called Calvary. The torn curtain, the quake, the tombs opening, those fallen asleep now raised up became a testimony, a revelation. Did they see it? Did they recognize the one who cried out?

We the by-standers of another era confess the plan laid out by God, the plan that offered us Jesus—the promise of resurrection.

164

We spend our lives in that knowledge and in balancing the challenges of our baptized life with the culture of our day, with the truth hidden among the voices of schemers. We are faced with a list—family, Church, personal vocation, politics, commandments, beatitudes, sacraments . . .

Yet, we are not alone on the stage. God's grace is peeking out, inviting us to accept the one who cries out in our behalf . . . . so that we too will be raised up on the last day!

7
Uncovering Dusters

For some reason my personality seems to invite people into my space. Those who visit me move about comfortably. They don't ask to open the refrigerator or a cupboard in search of an item not in plain sight. Actually, I enjoy that company would move about so freely.

My other space—what's going on with me—is entrusted to good friends . . . Oh, it's not in the sense of a careless telling all nor of holding some mystery when sharing time and stories with them. Now, in the face of two people separated in age I discovered a need for mystery.

Children are the ones who might cross the borders of privacy not realizing that everything personal or in hospitality or understanding are necessarily available to them. Thus we offer them Santa Clause, the Easter Bunny, the tooth fairy, the Stork to satisfy their inquisitive minds as they ramble through childhood.

My cousin Kay was seven. I was fourteen. It was during a usual family visit to our home. She, along with her brother, enjoyed their visits and their sense of wonderment would bring them to explore areas to see how our homes were different. Our breadbox interested them. Their mom was a well known baker in North Tonawanda and people loved her homemade cakes. But here in our home they asked "Aunt Sophie, do you have any store bought cupcakes?"

During one such exploration, Kay appeared in my bedroom. She was welcome in my space and I paid little attention until her discovery. She opened a drawer of my dresser. There lying in neat piles were the product of my recent graduation into young womanhood, the monthly need of a fourteen year old.

My response to her inquisition was quick—"Dusters, they're dusters". She was satisfied.

How am I to approach the parables of Jesus when he suggests "what is lain hidden will be revealed"? What does he mean "they look but do not see, and hear but do not understand"?

Jesus spoke in parables using the images, the everyday things in our lives. Those who listened were often like children seeking to understand. Sometimes they walked away confused. Still, Jesus did not pause to explain his message fully to them. And remember that we read that he drew the children to himself and that he said we should be as children. What did he say to the children? What did he say to those who heard him speak? . . . does he say to us?

Sometimes children break into our space. Their curiosity is openness to their surroundings and to the parables being offered them. Children may look and see and not perceive. We seem to hold them away from the fullness of understanding . . . feeding them, as it were, gently as we lead them toward the truth, breaking open the parables.

It seems that his stories are meant to urge them and us toward making parallels; that they be a part of an awakening faith. It is as though we are opening a drawer filled with life images and being drawn slowly toward knowledge of the mysteries, of an intimate space called the kingdom.

What was hidden will be revealed. In the meantime children experience a journey of faith reaching into reality for answers, probing that inner place where we may still have more to offer them.

Finally, they will uncover what it really was that satisfied them for a time—Santa Claus, the Easter Bunny, the tooth fairy, the Stork . . . and yes, the dusters.

Or it may be seeds, pearls, fig trees, weeds, yeast . . . . "many longed to see what you see . . . to hear what you hear . . . but did not".

14

The "Curse"

World War II was the curse that brought the United States into an allegiance with many European countries. Six long years of bloody conflict and the devastating curse of extermination on European Jews and Poles finally ended. It was 1945. Peace was restored.

I had been playing in our back yard when my mom rushed out to share the news with her daughter. My mom, a parachute inspector during those war years, was now the bearer of good news! It was news shared over a backyard fence or with passers by from the front porch. The curse had come to an end.

I remember other "good" news which she gladly shared with neighbors as she made her way to Lier's, the corner store. It was just a few years later. And the news was a mother's joy.

That news began . . . well, a little background first. It was the day when I found myself in the bathroom covering up a no no. How often was I told not to pick at a scab! And here I was blotting blood from the open scab on my leg. As you know, it takes time to stop the flow of blood on sensitive shins and especially when no band aids were on hand to treat this misbehavior. When I was there an unusually long time, my mom and aunt wondered why. I can guess their conversation. In a reaction, it was my aunt who came to the door. "Is there blood in the toilet?" she asked. Wow, how could she suspect? How was she aware of my bloody misdeed? In reality, her suspicions were directed to a young teen and about what has been called "the curse". No one had spoken to me about such a teen age event so she was concerned. In any event, there was no curse that day.

One day the curse did arrive. I was fourteen. My mom was alerted to the situation and she took over with a kind of pride in her developing daughter. Why do mothers find this event such an exciting one when all the world dubs it "the curse"?

Here I was, waiting for the help and lessons mom would provide. I peeked out the window and watched as she made her way to Lier's . . . to make the necessary purchase, the kind of protective "band aid" that will fulfill this first of monthly needs. Her trip was interrupted several times on route where women neighbors on porches heard the good news about her daughter's entry into the experience of womanhood.

The truth was out. I had no door to hide behind now. What was private now became public to those neighbors who smiled knowing something intimate about me . . . and that because of a mom bearing "good" news.

The book of Genesis reveals an episode of bad behavior and how a man and woman tried to hide their misdeeds behind fig leaves. The gardener God, ever aware of his creation, challenged them with a question and punished them with a curse.

Wait! As I reread the passage . . . who received the curse? It was the man upon whom a "curse" was proclaimed not the woman. Rather. God speaks about intensifying, meaning to make worse, what was already her experience—the woman's pain at childbirth. But, nothing about women's "monthly" or its being a punishment let alone a curse.

The curse was clearly made on the man. But read the curse—it is made on the ground because of him. It adds that he would need to toil and eat of the ground's plants until he returns to the ground from which he was taken. Then God says "for you are dirt/dust and to dirt/dust you shall return."

I find it interesting and wondered when it was that women looked at this natural event and accepted the menstrual flow as their "curse". Reading behind the lines—be fertile and multiply, offered me a thought. Did women begin to accept this monthly event as their inability to be fertile—the time when they were in-fertile? Was infertility their curse?

18

A Belated Birthday

On May 18, in 1990 or in many other years for that matter, a birthday tune sung in separate parts of the world and greeting two different celebrants. One might have heard "Happy Birthday dear Ruthy!" Another, "Happy Birthday dear Karol (or, dear Pope)!"

What do you think of that . . . a Campus Minister sharing a belated birthday with this man, this representative of Christ on earth!

Indeed there were differences between our May 18 births. We were separated by a generation, by our sex, and by our birthplaces. One thing in common was that we both came from a Polish heritage.

But in December 1990 the May birthday song, celebrations or gift giving had already passed. Instead, on this 10th day of December, I was in Rome and in a place where John Paul II was recognizing a special group of Pilgrims. Identified by blue scarves, these pilgrims were united as friends of Marguerite d'Youville, named "Saint" just one day before.

In Buffalo, on a nasty snow day, one day before flying to Rome, I had an inspiration. A gift for the Pope! What might it be? Aha! Another inspiration! Recalling our common birthdays I searched the possibility of purchasing a sweat shirt even on this snowy eve of departure. A sweat shirt because I knew the Pope took ski holidays. The chosen inscription was a logo that would announce a fact—"Happy Birthday—May 18th—Pope John Paul II and Sister Ruth Marie gnsh" . . . A belated gift!

175

Another "eve before" an event! The next day we would be privileged to have an audience with the Pope. I was excited about the gift I would give him. But this evening our pilgrim Grey Nuns from Buffalo challenged me as I modeled the blue sweat shirt with its greeting spelled out in large white letters. "How will you get it to him?" "Maybe there is a protocol!" Yikes! What protocol could I discover now, at ten o'clock at night?

So it was that the next day Paul, a Grey Nun Associate and I set out, gift in hand, ahead of our group to get an early front spot in line. The Swiss Guards were at the door so we approached them with our question—how to give the gift to the Pope. The answer "Just hand it to him." was a relief.

I remember the rush to find a place close to the aisle for my presentation and I remember the rush of my heart as the Pope neared me and my gift. Then it happened. As I offered the sweat shirt with a comment—"a birthday gift for you", he glanced at it as his associate accepted it for him. Still absorbed by the rush of emotion, I was aware of his hand on my head and his words of blessing—"Merry Christmas!" Merry Christmas! Spoken in English? Or Latin? Or was it Italian? No matter. The joy of the moment recognized the meaning.

Jesus' entry into Jerusalem on the back of a colt was heralded by palm waving crowds. He was arriving to offer an ultimate gift—it would be marked with the logo of a suffering servant, a crown of thorns, a cross. It would be his celebration—not of his birth thirty three years earlier.

Even on this part of his journey there would be others who would push forward from among those who wanted to be close, to call his name, to seek his healing touch. Now, they pushed forward to greet him with the logo of their grief.

Sometimes his disciples would try to pull Jesus away from them. But Jesus touched them, spoke to their need. Their joy was a response to the touch, to the words of healing.

Did they hear those words at all? "Come out of him . . . I rebuke the fever . . . your sins are forgiven . . . your faith has saved . . . I tell you arise . . . Power came out of me . . . You are set free . . . Be opened . . ." Or was it like a Merry Christmas wish, words lost in the joy of his touch, of his healing?

The response was certain and marked by immediacy—jumping up, standing up erect, responding to sight, words like incredible and amazing and expressions glorifying God. Some were physical and others verbal.

If the words of Jesus seemed lost, their meaning was recognized in the joy of their expressed responses.

31
The Funeral I Missed

Some friends and I were enjoying a seasonal get together when the topic arose. It was about a funeral, one that I obviously missed. It was about Sheila's friend Betsy who died several years before. They reminisced about the beautiful funeral service they had attended. What about me? Why was I not invited? They offered a response that was not satisfying to my understanding. I was certainly disappointed, although not angry that I missed that funeral.

I first knew Mini-Sheil's first West Highland. In fact I had met her with Sheila and shared many a day in their company in their South Buffalo home.

Sheila met an unnamed Mini, a scruffy, white, West Highland dog at the dog pond. We had gone there just "to look". As we started out to our destination, her mother had warned: "Don't bring home a dog!" Her warning went unheeded when Mini became a new member in their home.

Hearing the words "because you don't like dogs" did not make sense to me. True, when visiting the residents, I only greeted Mini with a pat and a dismissive "scat!"

And so it was with Betsy. She became a new member of the household now in its new home in Depew. Interesting that it was Betsy's funeral and not her birthday on Hallows Eve—31 October that became a remembered celebration. It was Mini's deceased relative that would now sadden Sheila's heart.

What are funerals about anyway? Aren't they times when one consoles those who are now bereft of one special to them? Certainly I would want to be present for Sheila as she experienced the loss of Betsy!

No invitation had been offered and I missed that funeral.

After that visit with friends, I reflected on the funeral I missed. I thought of the scriptural passage about the death of Lazarus and how Jesus missed a funeral. He lost his dear friend Lazarus. Mary and Martha, friends of Jesus, sisters of Lazarus, had informed him that Lazarus was ill. Jesus chose not to accept an invitation to come at once.

Rather, Jesus delayed his visit and when he arrived in Bethany, Lazarus was already in the tomb four days. According to Jewish customs Lazarus would have been buried the same day of his death. At the announcement Jesus wept. and the sisters wept knowing Jesus' presence would have saved their brother from death.

Ridden with grief, now they were in need of Jesus' comfort: "if you had been here . . ." Jesus' first consolation was "your brother will rise". Their response was one of faith, faith about resurrection on the last day. But the ultimate consolation he offered to the sisters in their mourning, in their acknowledging the reality of their brother's death was that they would "see the glory of God". The word was pronounced: "Rise!"

No, Jesus did not attend the funeral. Unlike my relationship with Sheil's pet, Lazarus was very dear to his sisters and to Jesus. Yet, his intentional delay resulted in people talking—suggesting that Jesus could have done something—after all he cured the blind.

I could not have offered my friend the assurance of a pet heaven—the hope of pet lovers. There would not be a resurrection for Betsy on the last day. Nor could I have pronounced "Rise!" had I been there.

I missed Betsy's funeral. I was not there to weep with my friend. My ultimate consolation for my dear friend who lost her dog would be recognized when she would have other Westies in her future, I would be there for those other dogs to pat and to dismiss with a "scat".

But above all I would have been there that day to mourn with my friend.

36

Come to the Table

How many tables can you name? The dining room and kitchen tables, coffee table, end table, accent table, console table, folding table, card table, picnic table, conference room table, gambling table, game table, tray table . . . ! Have I missed any?

We come to the table. The table—a piece of furniture designed to invite, to provide a space for gathering, for activities, for displaying objects!

Yet, the kitchen or dining room tables seem to be the ones that are the most versatile—inviting a variety of users for a variety of uses at a variety of times in a day!

It is the space where places are set for meals, often a casual gathering place for early morning or late night coffee chats, where the flat top may serve as a desk cluttered and with books or plans spread out there. Gamers come and remove the cloth covering and centerpiece décor and lay down their cards and coins for a time of fun or open a game board to challenge wits.

It is also the type of table found in restaurants where people gather to celebrate. So I invite you to come with me to a restaurant table designated for a celebration, for a celebrative meal and the unusual experience at this table.

It was the 100th anniversary of d'Youville College. Through a series of mix ups I was separated from my class of '62 members seated at table 4. I found myself at table 36 with the assurance that I would not be alone, that I would know one woman of the eight people assigned there. When I came to the table, there was only one person, a man, already seated and reading the program. I interrupted him to introduce myself. Then it happened! Our introductions revealed our identities and changed the celebration from a 100th anniversary celebration into a 64th year reunion of two classmates from the fourth grade at PS 42.

That providential occurrence created an excitement at our table, a rush of amazement that overflowed to others and changed the tone of our table for the evening. For Ed and Ruth our conversation became a time of remembering school days and school mates. And after the intended celebration of the evening came to an end, we left the table committed to a renewed friendship.

Table 36, set for a meal, had become a setting transformed for the unexpected!

The upcoming celebration had been a Jewish tradition for not 100 years but for hundreds.

We reflect on how the disciples went out to find a place and to prepare a Passover table. They heeded the direction of Jesus the one whom they called master, teacher. He is the one who, earlier, had questioned them about his identity: "Who do the crowds say that I am?" Answers came quickly, "John the Baptist," "Elijah," "One of the ancient prophets." Though the responses were wrong, their leader was being touted as someone they held in high esteem.

When Jesus turned the question on them, he hoped to draw out the disciples' personal experience of him. "But who do you say that I am?" It is Peter who gets it right: "the Christ of God."

Now Peter and the others gathered at table with Jesus. There was no surprise at being at the Passover table with their charismatic leader, the Christ of God. There was no rush of excitement to further identify Jesus. So what happened at that table was rather a time of reverence, of awe. It became a time when "remembering" would be their commission. They too must remember to wash the feet of others. They too must pronounce the words "This is my body . . . my blood." "When you do this remember me."

The table, set for a Passover meal had become the setting where the unexpected happened, where bread and wine were transformed, and over 2000 years later we still remember, we do this in "remembrance of me".

43
"I Felt Bad!"

We had played table tennis the day before" she recalled. "When I heard about your broken legs, I felt bad about that game." The memory of that event, and of other "I remember when" chatting, happened during a 150th anniversary celebration when the two of us met among the guests gathered at the reception.

The thing was that it was our first meeting in 43 years. Janet had long ago chosen to leave the convent and our lives had taken different directions—mine to assignments in a variety of schools and cities and she as a nurse finally settling in Georgia. Now in Buffalo she had come as an HAA alumna on this anniversary of the academy.

Janet picked me out from among the guests and we must have talked for an hour. Janet was a novice when I, a postulant, had been diagnosed with having two fine line leg fractures. She offered the memory of the table tennis game and of how we had met at another game in another time.

It was our very first meeting. It took place before either of us had entered the convent. I was a CYO basketball coach and had annoyed her team with a tactic that led to their defeat. It seems that I had connected with my players with a song. When verses were sung out they called for particular plays—or annoyed enough—and our ultimate win.

But in that particular postulant experience when I returned from the hospital visit with a cast on one leg and a crutch to relieve the other, poor Janet really felt bad and it wasn't her fault at all.

I did remind her of another time before the table tennis game. My legs with a yet to be diagnosed reason for pain, were already hurting me. One day as we passed each other on the stairs we exchanged what might be called a chant. It is the refrain that one offers casually: "Hi how are you?" And the expected response: "Fine and you?" That day however my response "I am hurting" surprised her and she continued on after a simple "Oh!" Like the years before at that CYO game, I had caused her some confusion.

I find it interesting on how we store memories of our experiences with others. Who would have thought that forty three years and more would raise these two events—both involved with playing games and how each game was followed with unexpected endings.

Passover. A time to celebrate an anniversary! Scripture reminds us of how twelve had gathered with Jesus for this time of remembering. It was an anniversary event.

Passover was the reminder of God's saving event thousands of years before. They would raise up that memory, that story retold of how their ancestors were told to slay the lamb, to share the lamb for a meal and to splash their doors with the blood of the lamb and all in the household would be saved.

The apostles had been with Jesus for three years. Certainly that time together began to store a variety of memories for each of them and likely they would have shared them. They were their lived experience of times together.

Now, as the disciples sit with Jesus the memory takes on a new shape. The words of the refrain are sounded, echoes of their ancestral event—lamb, eat, drink, blood. The elements would be on the table. But there would be an unexpected ending.

188

Jesus tells them to eat: "This is my Body" . . . drink: "This is my Blood".

How did the disciples respond to this new ending? How did they feel? Was there confusion? Scripture only recounts that they ate and drank. But one among them who ate and drank missed something because his response was to leave the table.

Do you think he left the table missing what Jesus had just chanted over bread and wine? Unexpected words!

Do you think his response to unexpected words, like many of ours, might also have been a simple "Oh!"?

90
A Bungee Ride!

The last thing I expected as I looked toward the Grey Nun Associate Pilgrimage was a bungee ride. I, a convener of a group of GNSHA, would be joining this group of thirty seven Associates and a number of Grey Nuns for a gathering. The pilgrimage would bring us to step into the history of our founder St. Marguerite d'Youville—Isle St. Bernard, Chateauguay! Maison de Mere d'Youville, Montreal! Her birthplace in Varennes and St. Ann's Church! What a wonderful experience it promised to be!

The pilgrimage days were extended as my companion, Al John, gnsha, and I, did a bit more of history seeking. We enjoyed an excursion to the Khawanokee reservation and St. Francis Church. It was part of the mission established by St. Francis Xavier. Al John and I belonged to St. Francis Xavier parish in Buffalo before a recent merge of churches. At this St. Francis we prayed before the remains of Kateri Tekawetha which were returned there, her home, from the United States. It reminded us of how soon Marguerite's remains would be in her new home, a transfer from the Motherhouse on Guy Street to Varennes. A place in the church of her baptism there had an area awaiting her arrival.

Our excursion ended by a visit to the Motherhouse on Guy Street where we enjoyed a tour directed by a dear, Sr. Marguerite, sgm.

A bungee ride! Neither the Associate pilgrimage plans nor our personal pilgrimage charted a bungee ride. So, where in the experience of these memorable places did our bungee experience happen?

When we started back to Buffalo we activated the GPS and off we went for a smooth trip. Until . . . . we stopped for coffee at a McDonald's on the I-90 in NY a few hours from home. As I backed away from McDonald's I heard an awful crunch. The front of my Toyota Yaris caught on the curb (don't know how) and the front panel broke away, Well, Al John was able to lift it but the bolts (probably plastic) that held it were gone. But never fear . . . this ol' nun always carries a bungee cord with her. Why??? So our creative genes were activated and we joined the front body panel to a piece under the hood. Thus we traveled home safely to Buffalo on our memorable . . . bungee ride.

PS
Oh, did I forget to tell about being lost between Montreal and Chateauguay, twice caught in the unbridled traffic on the Champlagne Bridge . . . about a stop for lunch at Charley's when we finally reached Chateauguay? About loosing my cell phone somewhere along the way? Another unexpected incident!

––––––––––––––––––

The places where Jesus walked have become places of pilgrimage. Two thousand years ago, they were simply the places where this controversial man passed by or paused to share God's word.

His mother birthed him in a manger and welcomed shepherds and Magi on their pilgrimage. He could be found near the River Jordan being baptized by John and teaching often near the lake or on hillsides. He grew up in Nazareth but it was not a place that welcomed his return. There was his arrival in Jerusalem amid the palms waving a welcome. A Jew, Jesus went to a place to celebrate a Passover meal. One of the important places in Jesus' pilgrimage was what we now call the Via Dolorosa—the sad road, the Stations of the Cross.

All were a part of a yet uncharted history. Scripture, paintings, relics and statues depict the scenes, reveal the story of God walking among the people. God—made man—made a pilgrimage from the manger to the cross.

Today, pilgrims arrive in the Holy Land eager to step into Jesus' history. Perhaps they hesitate as they pause to reflect on the horror represented by a hill, that place where Jesus was lifted up on a cross. Perhaps they realize that there was no bungee cord to support the broken body of Jesus, hanging there on his way home to the Father.

Al John and I ended our pilgrimage safely because of the simple support of that bungee cord.

100

The Menu

Buffalo folks love to eat! If Buffalo has been recognized as a city diminished in size or as the snow capital, it must also be hailed for its food. Just as the postal department proclaims a motto of nothing stops delivery, so our fair city lets nothing stop residents from getting out there and finding their favorite menu.

And, favorite menus there are! In this multi cultural city one can find the food that best satisfies his palate. That satisfaction is realized in our many restaurants, in the many events that sponsor specialty quizzinne, as well as the many popular tastes of Buffalo. Name the season or ethnic holiday and Buffalonians have a reason to seek out food. Thus, we find places like the popular Broadway Market!

A small band of Buffalo friends made a pact—to gather monthly at our homes for a meal together. One month this pact brought us to 100 Amherst Street, the home of Bruce and Karen.

What would the menu be? We sat down and our chef-hosts handed us a written menu. Wow! A written menu! In addition to the menu, the hosts advised us that we would be served a la carte, one item at a time and individually according to each person's menu selection.

It was with excitement that I took a first look. The items listed were not the expected names. Rather, each was hidden in a non-recognizable description. At the same time we noticed the absence of utensils on the table. Aha! They too were on the menu, disguised among the multi items listed.

I'd like to invite you to "experience" the meal. Check the menu that follows and how your meal will be served a la carte. A reminder—Be sure to order utensils first (if you can find them)! If you are stumped, just check with Bruce and Karen to see if they will unveil their mystery menu. Or better yet, ask to be invited to their hospitable meal . . . and to their friendship as well—the real gift, a prize, behind the menu.

A band of 12 had gathered for an ethnic celebration—Passover. Scripture reminds us that the disciples "did as Jesus ordered, and prepared the Passover". Now they were at table with Jesus. We can imagine the scene. Yet, neither Scripture nor art has ever described what was on the table on that feast day. No mention is made of the expected menu, the food that was to be placed on the table.

Tradition presents the Jewish menu for a Seder meal: 3 matzos, wine and a symbolic plate of maror, charoset, beitzah, karpas, and zeroah. Unfamiliar names to some of us. Traditional food known by the disciples! Had they provided all the food?

A cup of wine and of the 3 matzos, tradition has it that one is kept until the end of the meal, as a prize.

When we envision the scene with the disciples at table with Jesus, we become aware of Jesus' prize for them—a menu for life hidden as matzo—unleavened bread—and some wine.

Yes, a prize, a surprise offered—after the meal with the wine and the one matzo. that Jesus was giving the disciples, and through them to each of us. A prize—his menu, the gift of his Body and Blood!

Passover Menu

Maror-bitter herbs
Charoset: A sweet, brown, pebbly paste of fruits and nuts
Karpas: A vegetable other than bitter herbs, usually parsley
Zeroah: A roasted lamb
Beitzah: A roasted egg
Matzoh: unleavened bread

The Woody Menu

Please order your entire meal at one time and observe the following:

1. No peeking at your neighbor's choices. Make your own mistakes.
2. Each item may be ordered only once.
3. One course will be served a la carte exactly in the order written on your order.
4. One course must be completed before your next item will be served.
5. Emily Post's rules of etiquette definitely do not apply.

This dinner was planned for one reason only—to have fun!
Here are the selections. So, enjoy yourself!

Lover's Delight . . . . Royal's Rival . . . . Bug's choice . . . . Neptune's
Helper . . . . Molar Digger

Royce's Partner . . . . Dracula's Delight . . . .
Sleeping Relative . . . .

Bad Actor with Irish Eyes . . . . Newport's Life . . . .
"Mr. S's" Drippings . . . .

Stringy Skinny Helper . . . . Mt. McKinley . . . .
Wilkinson's Edge . . . . Musical Fruit . . . .

Popeye's Amour . . . . Pucker Power . . . . Drunken Delmonte

Number each in the order you want to be served . . .
a plate is provided for starters—
see translation at end of this book

200

The Bag Lady

Have you ever watched a homeless woman—a "bag lady" as she trudges down the street? I think you can picture her as she pushes a borrowed shopping cart of the K-Mart or Target ilk. The cart is full . . . plastic bags holding the extent of private belongings, all she owns; filled with a variety of other items including pop cans which might be exchanged for a small amount of cash.

Harsh weather reveals a picture of the woman wearing the layers of clothing, clothing not appropriate for Buffalo's worst winters, but unmatched piece upon piece from that plastic closet in her cart.

It gives me pause to see the scene and to wonder about her life. What did she do "before", in another life? Why is she walking our streets? Where does she find respite from weather, rest for the night or just a place "to be"? I suppose she knows where to stop for a meal. But loitering? Is she always on the move?

Let me tell you about a particular "bag lady", one I met over fifteen years ago. She grew up, a farm girl in a large family. She experienced college and teaching and working for the county. Now retired, Joyce looks at old pictures of family, children and now grandchildren. One picture reveals her in bathing suit ready for beauty contest finals. Her first ambitions—modeling and singing on stage in musical comedy were not fully realized. Undaunted, Joyce found a place for music in her life. For many years she has offered her beautiful voice singing in her church music ensemble.

Joyce is my "bag lady". These days she shuffles along with what she refers to as "my trolley cart". She removes her cart from the trunk of her car. It is a walker that aids her as she meets the challenges of the day burdened with arthritis. My bag lady also lugs a bag—well some might call it a purse. That bag, I have discovered, weighs about fifteen pounds. I challenged Joyce to count the items in her bag. After a hesitation she admitted: "two hundred (on average)"! I was overwhelmed by the number and the variety of items—not one calendar but two, not one change purse but two, a variety of plastic bags each with it's particular contents, cosmetic case (with seven items), coupons for stores and restaurants, a large snap purse with items such as greeting cards . . . and on and on.

Joyce spends many days on the streets, her trolley in front, bag in hand, destination marked on her calendar. Her destinations are to those places where she offers hours of ministry to the service of others. It may be radio reading for the blind, or collecting personal items for the boys at a Franciscan home. It may be hours accepting pledges for kids escaping drugs. Perhaps you met Joyce at the Kazoo Fest table where sales were to benefit Camp Good Days. Frequently, she pauses and reaches into her bag. There she finds the card, the stamp and the envelope with some money in it and makes a gift to some place where someone will be fed—physically, emotionally, spiritually.

Picture them. Jesus and his disciples, itinerants, walking along the seaside and through small towns along the way! Perhaps they appear to be a "bag lady" type. After all Jesus and his disciples left home, had no where to lay their head and to have only the sandals they were wearing. We see them at the homes of others being provided a meal and the courtesy of having the traditional foot wash to remove the dust accumulated during their walk.

As they walked along, one among them was carrying a wicker basket, a kind of "bag" filled with five loaves and two fishes. Were these the left-overs from a recent visit? Was this their meager provision for an evening meal? Just enough for their small group?

But when the crowds saw them and began following them, Jesus took pity on them and ministered to their needs. When it grew late the disciples were concerned that the crowd might be hungry. They had their five loaves and two fishes. At Jesus' command they emptied their baskets to feed the hungry crowds. Then there were left-overs.

Do bag ladies walking along our streets empty their plastic bags to share the contents? Or must they too seek out those who minister to their needs and who offer them sustenance at places like "Loaves and Fishes" or "Friends of the Night People" or . . . ? Like the crowds that received the generosity of Jesus and his disciples, there are those who make offerings that provide for others out of their own small sustenance . . . enough to provide an evening meal

I am privileged to know such a "bag lady". Joyce, who reaches into her fifteen pound bag, selects her change purse or checkbook from among two hundred items and from her small retirement resources makes a gift. From out of that bag Joyce—my friend, and Grey Nun Associate, offers her hands to the needy.

At the end of the day she finds respite in a lounge chair where she can just "be".

1750

German Chocolate

Guests would be arriving—an entourage of Grey Nuns from Canada. Their visit was for the business of a leadership gathering of the five congregations of Grey Nuns. They would arrive the next morning to our Motherhouse on 1750 Quarry Road.

Many of us have had the experience of out of town visitors. Don't we always do our best to make them extra comfortable? Even if it takes a bit more of our time or energy! And even if we are not nuns expecting visitors!

These visitors would require hospitality and Sr. Mary Raphael would be sure that it would be the best, one befitting our welcoming reputation. "Raph", our affectionate nickname for this very holy person, assembled a group of sisters for the multiple tasks involved. There were room cleaning, beds to make, and comfort accessories provided for each room.

It was a busy late afternoon for this crew of sisters. The tasks were ones we, or other sisters, had performed for other occasions of welcoming visitors. We accomplished all by early evening and despite the pressing heat of that summer day.

Raph praised us for our work and then offered us a delicious reward. Ice cream! Goodnoe's ice cream! Sr. Marge and I would drive there and bring back the cool treat. She prepared a list naming the sister and her choice flavor.

At Goodnoe, Sister Marge was calling out the selections. The server suggested, "Just give me the list, it will be easier." After a bit she called out, "We have no German chocolate." But no one had asked for German chocolate. A review of the list exposed the error and brought a round of laughter to us and to the sisters when we returned with the ice cream and retold the episode.

The list read: Sr.Mary Germaine, chocolate!

We are familiar with the many parables of Jesus recorded in the Gospels. Jesus spoke to his listeners and to his disciples with this mode of revealing his message. He even says he will speak in parables so as to announce what lay hidden—even from the foundation of the world.

Though the parables used were common to the people—fig trees, weeds, yeast, mustard seeds . . .—their meaning was often not as clear. They required an explanation because they just didn't get it.

The server at Goodnoe didn't get it either when she read our flavor parable. It took an explanation to reveal the meaning of the message.

One such time Jesus was speaking to his disciples telling them to beware the "leaven" of the Pharisees and Sadducees. The disciples discussed among themselves that it was because they had not brought bread. Jesus admonishes them for their lack of faith. He tells them that's not the message or the reason. He reminds them of the few loaves of bread and how there were leftovers after feeding thousands and the real message of the miracles.

Aha! They now caught on. They understood that Jesus was not telling them to beware of the "leaven of bread". What he meant was beware the "teaching" of the Pharisees and the Sadducees.

Do we get it when life's list of concerns comes at us hidden in the parables of our culture?

1939

"... down Mexico Way"

Strains of the cowboy song came to mind as I remembered my trips south of the border, down Mexico way. The song was first popularized by Gene Autry in 1939 and the romantic lyrics were sung by Sinatra, Englebert, and Cline among others. But today it is a different romance that flows as the lyrics become personal for me—It is the love of a Spanish professor to recall her experiences of the culture and language she has taught over many years. So, "now as I wander my thoughts ever stray, south of the border down Mexico way".

The first trip south of the border was a day trip with Campus Ministers that allowed a first hand look at the hundreds of illegal immigrants scrambling across the border their activity cloaked by the dark night sky. My encouraging cheers:" go for it"—have changed radically over the years . . .

1996: A three city vacation adventure, a prize claimed by a friend and the first leg taking us to Mazatlan (Jan.7-9). On the 10th an 8 hour bus trip began at 9pm for a trip to Puerto Vallarta (Jan. 11th and 12th). A flight on the Mexicana took us to Zihuantanejo-Ixtapa. We were typical tourists visiting sights, in a pulmonia (golf cart type taxi), enjoying the beaches, participating in an outdoor Mass facing a Pacific sunset, enjoying special dinners and cruise rides and even an "ultra-light" ride high above the towering beach hotels. These and more activities were parceled into two days in each city followed by a days travel to the next.

"South of the border . . . I went back one day". It is a small world. I found an address that led me to a former teacher at Cardinal

Dougherty High School on Amherst Street. He was working in San Diego. Through his contact and efforts I was able to 'go back', return, not one day but twice for a week each.

Those weeks during January I crossed the San Diego border into Mexico. I traveled to an area where I met sisters who were serving at La Esperanza (Hope), a clinic located on a high colina overlooking Tijuana. The clinic and its offering of healing were unlike the poverty and squalor, the dumps crawling with pouching birds that surrounded it and the muddy road leading to it.

And I? I became part of the hope and healing promised by this clinic. My task was simple—to arrange the pharmacy, translate the directions on donated medicines and to fill the scripts provided for patients by visiting doctors.

In the sisters' convent behind the clinic I became part of their life—sharing meals, companionship, prayer times and local outdoor Masses. I tutored Sr.Ines, a doctor, with her English and accompanied her for home visits and to Tijuana to secure clothing and other donations from a St. Vincent de Paul donation center there.

When the time came to leave after my second experience at La Esperanza, like the sad lyrics that promised "mañana" I rode away and "I whispered mañana" but "mañana" never came . . .

———————

"Come back to me with all your heart, don't let fear keep you apart . . ." When we sing the words at Mass I am reminded of Hosea's prophetic message. He was urging an unfaithful Israel to return to God, to do right and always hope in him.

And then I picture Jesus proclaiming a message of love on a mountain where he offers the beatitudes as the way to do right.

The strains of that song continue at Mass—"long have I waited for your coming home to me . . ." Can you almost hear Jesus singing this message of his ministry along with us? Yes, Jesus, present with God, as God from the beginning. Jesus the long awaited Messiah singing about our 'today'. And what is our response? How many times do we whisper "mañana"?

The message bearers, the song, continue to urge: return to me with all your heart—'now'. What is our refrain? Do we sing the response of that other song? "Mañana"?

1980

Someone Stepped In

The best laid plans . . . are often not appreciated. Where is it that they break down? I cannot remember the first signs.

Yes, I took the ministry assignment as a call, one to respond to a need for a principal in a small town catholic school. I was eager to develop a preparedness for the position that was a bit outside of my background as a high school Spanish teacher, elementary teacher of English and Math, and new student of Theology at the Seminary. Nevertheless, I reached out to a summer of readiness to take a quick study of principal preparation classes. There I experienced some success as a class leader and even implemented that leadership in the last day event. It was a creative use of the learned principles in a social to end classes just before going off to our respective school assignments! A success!

But, on arrival I was still not aware of any foreboding signs, I took on my task with a positive attitude and an awareness of my surroundings from kid studies, pranks, and uniforms, to school program advances, to faculty and staff assignments, to bus regulations. And yes, even an after school wine and cheese faculty social to assure our camaraderie as catholic educators on the same team. Always, I was aware of my role in these matters.

Despite good intentions and the positive elements and outcomes in each of those, there lay an undercurrent of objection to change. Two camps each—of parents and of faculty/staff. The burden fell heavily upon me and became one difficult to bear in the silence of the negative camps.

Then someone stepped in. Was it my new and dear friend Nat, my school secretary and parish Confirmation "boss"? The words came when she indicated "I signed you up for a weekend program—Cursillo! Cursillo? That is intended for initiation in the faith (much like a four day tour of the rite of Christian initiation . . . RCIA) or the mature development of one's faith mostly for lay men and women. Cursillo? Me? A religious sister?

The weekend was filled with the unexpected—the sharing, the prayer, the teasing by new associates, the leadership including a priest friend, the letters of support and the arrival of the support community of cursillistas bellowing "De Colores". All unexpected! And, we were introduced to a new song . . . On Eagles' Wings. It became our, or at least my, theme song for the weekend. Its words rushed through me: "And He will raise you up on eagles' wings . . . and hold you in the palm of His hand."

It was a time when I was lifted up . . . felt the support that surrounded me—people, music, community . . . and my God.

Yes, I felt the support of all present and even where my table group accepted my suggested name "Las Verdes", the green ones. Yes there was a place for a religious sister in this Cursillo experience.

The whole sense and assurance of community, of the people of God gathered, of loving acceptance, rose out of this four day encounter. It was a time when somehow in the midst of faith building, of learning and experiencing "Church" that I encountered more than the outward mission of Cursillo. It was in the atmosphere of its "De Colores" that its words reached my heart with an unexpected color:

Joyous, joyous
Let us live in grace since we can.
Let us quench, let us quench the burning thirst of the
King who does not die.
Joyous, joyous
Let us bring to Christ a soul and thousand more.
Spreading the light that illuminates the divine grace from
the great ideal.
Spreading the light that illuminates the divine grace from
the great ideal
And that is why I love the great loves of many colors
And that is why I love the great loves of many colors.**

Someone stepped in. Someone reached into my heart, raised me up and I was able to take His hand and joyously move on in my journey, spreading the light that illuminates.

St. John's Gospel reaches beyond the synoptic tales of Jesus' birth and exposes the rich plan of God, a plan drawn from the moment of creation. "In the beginning was the Word" he proclaims . . . not the arrival of gift bearing Magi. Rather, it is the gift of Logo that he reveals, Logo, Word. In the Christmas of creation, John continues: "what came to be through him was life and this life was the light of the human race". The Logo, God's Word, stepped in before the world began.

Before God's creative Word was uttered there was chaos. Everything would soon be drawn together in a movement that began with his Word: "Let there be light."

There followed what might be called the de colores of creation. That very light is the powerful grace that urges us, which John says is life and that the life-light shines in the darkness that cannot now overcome it.

In the experience of Cursillo someone stepped in and the darkness did not overcome the light.**

** [The song De Colores is sung by Angicaro (a saintly character) in Alison Mackie's novel The Gypsy Chronicles. The power and grace of De Colores moves through a bus like a wave, and it is not long before everyone, including an unsavory gang of thugs trying to cause trouble, are holding hands, singing and swaying in the tradition of De Colores, brought together in spirit by the song's powerful grace.]

2001

A Beer in Bolivia

Lake Titicaca was in view, boats bobbing on its brilliant blue surface. Here, on the lawn of the Maryknoll house I stood with a bottle of beer in hand and a rush of campus minister photo takers ready for . . . .

Well, first let me identify that group. We were twenty two campus ministers who had quickly become a community when we shared our first days at Maryknoll in Lima, Peru. It was June 2000. We had come from a variety of college campuses between California and New York. And I, from ECC—City in Buffalo New York. The youngest at 22 was an assistant Campus Minister bubbling with the ideas of youth. The oldest, an 82 year old religious brother was tied to traditional modes of expression. We were indeed a motley group who came from motley campuses who came to experience "Campus Ministry Across the Americas".

Partying and sharing conversations those first days in Lima was responsible for the closeness that developed among us and many of our idiosyncrasies became the stuff of our playfulness.

Thus the group discovered that I had never drunk a beer. No, not even though my parents were beer drinkers as were relatives, friends and dates who often imbibed as well. After much ribbing, somehow there came a group consensus: "Ruth will have a beer—her first—in Bolivia".

It was thus that our arrival in Bolivia was filled with photo taker anticipation. I was urged onto the lawn, beer in hand, to consecrate the event—yes even with a single slug and multiple memories to

213

be placed in scrapbooks . . . somewhere, for sometime searched memories.

That event was bested by the reason for, and the experiences we shared on this, a first Maryknoll offering for Campus Ministers. Uncomfortable busses, somewhat akin to what we know locally as "cheesies" brought us safely city to city and to a variety of university campuses. There we were introduced to the history and lived culture and entertainment presented by academia and students. We found ourselves embedded in the midst of that history and culture as we climbed the heights of Machu Pichu, ran our hands against the walls of brick in Puno, shopped in natives' open markets, and enjoyed stops that offered us the tastes of music, dance and food.

But, ne'er another beer . . . only a sip of South America!

My recent involvement in the study of Matthew's gospel took me on a different journey. The gospel reveals how Jesus' journeys took him across first century Palestine from Bethlehem to the area around the Sea of Galilee and to the lowest point on the earth.

His was a spiritual journey that would unlock the mystery of the awaited Messiah if only his own Jewish people—Jewish scriptural photo takers—would allow themselves to be embedded in his message. Then they might recognize in his journey and ministry the parallel images of Israel and Jesus and their struggles for liberty.

Like their ancestors of old who sought freedom from captivity, the Palestinian heirs of Israel sought liberation—to be free from Roman domination. Jesus stood, where Israel had stood before him. Now he stood ready to release the people from their captivity, to liberate them from their sin.

Jesus presented himself to them, a New Covenant in his hand, inviting them to be immersed in a new holiness. His hands were nailed to the cross bars of his sacrifice. And the onlookers—the photo takers—now hold their memories in the pages of an old or a new covenant.

But, ne'er another Messiah . . . only the taste of His Body and Blood!

2012

Good Friday

Fridays are my good days . . . usually. Then there was "that" Friday that began with all good plans in order: morning prayer, an email check over coffee and cinnamon bread, noon Mass downtown and then off to my fifth year of radio reading at the Niagara Frontier Radio Reading Service for the visually impaired. Added to the good of the day was using a coupon at Delta Sonic—reduced wash and interior cleaning. All accomplished by 4 pm.

I looked forward to a two hour respite at home and my 6 pm pick up of a fellow traveler. Then a 20 mile highway jaunt to Lewiston and a 6:30 wonderful philosophy class! Or, so I thought.

Bad news seeped in to interfere with a Good Friday plan. The car clean-up revealed a large bulge on the rear tire of the car. And the advice: "Drive slowly and avoid bumps; keep off highways; don't drive over 30 mph; get a new tire"! So much for a "good" Frida

Time was rushing by: 4:30 no tire at local Car Garage! 4:45 aha! 5:30 a new "Dunn" tire and a bill hinted at return to a good Friday.

The unexpected—now good news entered "when I was looking". It was in the midst of an "itchy wait" in the waiting room of that Dunn Tire. The events of the day had brought me to this place where I stared at the unusual pattern of the wallpaper. White! In a place like this? White with small black fleur de leis dotting its three white walls!

As I stood to pay the bill, I began to chat with John about the wallpaper. Now why would I be moved to bother him with talk about wallpaper? And, why didn't he know it was white with fleur de leis? And why did I point to the fleur de leis on my crucifix to inform him of what they were? His response had nothing to do with wallpaper or crucifixes. Rather he blurted out "I was never baptized". Wallpaper gave way to a conversation about Church and faith and wanting to be baptized and marry in Church. My suggestions were offered about Mass and baptism catechesis . . . But it is a providential God and Holy Spirit who were in charge of this Friday.

The "bulging tire" incident interrupted my hope for an anticipated respite. Rather, something new, something good was offered near that white wallpaper with the fleur de leis.

Was that indeed a return to my Good Friday? Now, a wonderful philosophy class remained to make this Friday good. But . . . .

. . . it happened on the highway. The screeching sound of a broken belly shield rubbing against the front tire caused us to stop. After our amateur diagnosis and temporary bungee cord repair effort we arrived late for our favorite philosophy class. And Providence and the Holy Spirit? What was in their mind now?

We call it "Good Friday". Yet the scene presents us with nothing that appears good. Oh, the day before was filled with good. Jesus' plan was to share the gift his body and blood and to introduce the twelve to the meaning of service. It was the plan of the future Church leadership and of a commission to "feed my sheep". Soon evil would seep into that gathering and later a midnight kiss—not of love but betrayal. A holy day was moving from the darkness and into the wee hours of a bad Friday.

That Friday Jesus experienced physical and emotional trauma. There was a crown of thorns pressed against a bleeding brow, deep slashes wrapped around and cut his innocent body, and the burden of a cross was laid heavy against his shoulders. Finally, there would be nails driven into his consecrating hands.

How did he feel as he appeared in this public, tortured posture? What was he thinking as shouts proclaimed him a criminal and named the penalty—"Crucify him!"? What did he think about his friends who cowered in denial of knowing him? Did it hurt him to watch his mother ache with his pain?

I remember a five year old who was found kneeling near a cross with the crucified Christ. She simply acknowledged: "Jesus sure had a bad day". A bad day! Clarissa, a child, looked and identified the obvious.

A bad day! And us? Do we stare at the background of a cross and see the image painted on its wood and see its meaning?

But there were those two bad Fridays—33 AD and 2012 AD—each with an intervening event. In the mystery of a loving God they became "good"—the doors of heaven opened to invite us in and a conversation about wallpaper opened another door.

2049

Permanent Waves

I rushed to the vestry after Mass, well kind of since my walker has some control over my speed. The vestry is the place where the priest vests, that is dresses or robes for the Mass. There he was, Fr. Bob, slightly built, face a bit older and hair now white and loosely tossed. Yes, years had passed since our last meeting but the physical changes still left him a handsome man and a friend recognizable in our quick embrace.

No question at all that this was the Bob of my past when he began to quip and tease exhibiting his trademark humor. We stood near the door doing some catch up conversation. I was pleased to hear he had read my book, "The Scoop on Ruth", and enjoyed it. Of course, typically Bob, he was quick to note that I had omitted him from among my tales. Well, I assured him I could include him in my second book which I was completing soon.

A Fr. Bob event rushed quickly to mind but which I did not divulge at the time. But, you asked for it Bob so here goes.

That day some years ago, I was driving past the Church on the right. I continued on and, finally arriving down the road on the left, I entered 2049 for a quick visit.

My brother, a hair dresser, welcomed me into the house. At the time, he had his salon business in the attached garage which sported the name "The Matador". I had provided him with an authentically dressed matador mannequin so the name had an appropriate "living" (so to speak) logo.

221

After a bit, he became a bit devilish and said I should peek into the salon saying, "you'll wish you had a camera." I opened the door cautiously, not knowing what to expect. I howled at the sight! There, seated in the chair, was Fr. Bob not in expectation of a barber's trim of his full dark hair but in the mid process of getting a permanent wave. He tried to hide the evidence of this hair curling adventure but it was too late. I had caught him. No camera! But the memory never faded.

Now, near the vestry door I was standing with a white haired priest whose only remnant of a permanent wave is a life of priesthood, an ordination offering a <u>permanent wave</u> beginning long ago with the anointing of his hands.

I end this with the permanent memory of the priest, the matador and his permanent wave. Yes, I laughed at the figure of a priest posed in an awkward situation seated on a beauty salon chair.

There was another priest, in another time, who was posed against a cross, a criminal's domain of punishment . . . Jesus.

Scripture records the words of mockery: the revolutionary criminal hanging near him challenged his claim; passers by reviled him; the chief priests, scribes and elders mocked his claim to be king.

Words of disdain were being proclaimed. But there were other words, ones the hecklers failed to hear, words that an Eternal God provided as a permanent wave that would affect us forever.

Genesis records that God spoke, and all creation came to be by his Word. John reminds us: "In the beginning was the Word, and the Word was with God, and the Word was God." When Jesus was baptized in the Jordan, God affirmed that relationship with Jesus calling him "my beloved Son".

Yet, as Jesus spent his years teaching God's word, proclaiming justice and offering compassionate healing, that message, the eternal Word of God posed against the cross would seem to have lost a sense of its permanence. Rather, at this vestry of heaven, Jesus—priest, prophet and king—entered via the cross and covered with the blood of disdain, thus fulfilling Gods permanent commitment to us for our salvation.

3410

Stalking?

We drove along the Pacific Coast Hwy. I could hardly believe I was in Malibu, Ca. as I glanced at the Pacific Ocean that paralleled us on the left and the roads opening and rising up into the Santa Monica Mountains on our right. We turned onto Serra Road and into a gated community.

I didn't know who the residents might be living in this community as we continued up Serra Road, past many break away roads revealing huge homes and estates. Our drive wove along the road to our destination atop a 23 acre knoll and the Serra Retreat Center at 3410 Serra Road.

Here a group of Campus Ministers had come away from our campuses, had responded to the call to "come apart and rest a while" (Mk.6:31) and to be transformed. We were welcomed in the Franciscan spirit of the place, by the unbelievable view of the ocean and mountains, and by the unrelenting heat of four July days. Bedroom fans provided the only relief from the heat. There were no fans or air conditioning in any other rooms.

Thus the "Transform Retreat' began on a hot July 25th. The heat was taking a particularly difficult toll on me as I walked from meeting room to dining room to chapel—walked in and out of the indoor and outdoor areas of the center.

Was Chrysta bothered by the heat as much as I or was she being her usual thoughtful self when she made a great suggestion during a break time on day two? "Let's take a ride around the community". A ride meant air conditioning. How could I refuse!

Chrysta chauffeured us through several of those break away roads that we had passed a day earlier. Did she know something that I didn't? that movie stars lived in this gated community? We drove past homes, parking and hoping to catch sight of stars. Were we just being curious or were we stalkers? Or pavarotti? No matter, our curiosity or stalking resulted in pictures of their homes—proof of our experience for a later excited sharing with others. "I never saw Mel Gibson but I took a picture of his house", I'd proclaim. But the thrill of that ride was when Dick Van Dyke parked near his home. I jumped out of the car and called out a greeting and told him I enjoyed his TV shows. He waved and offered a thanks. My heart beat with excitement.

The heat never broke and my intention to remain at the Center after the retreat changed—not from plans for stalking stars but to get home to a refreshing, cooler Buffalo.

Jesus had invited the Apostles to "come away to a deserted place and rest a while". They had just returned from a journey. It was their mission—their work was driving out demons and anointing the sick with oils and curing them. Now they sought a place of rest. But people found out and got to that place ahead of them. There was no gated community to halt their approach to that place where the Apostles and Jesus claimed for rest.

Scripture does not say how much rest they got after all. Unlike my attack by heat, they were overwhelmed by the crowds who sought after them. Were they curious or were they stalking them?

Soon the Apostles had another task—"Give them some food yourselves", Jesus said.

Like the Apostles, we all spend our time, our lives on a "journey". It is the daily work we do as Campus Ministers, or laborers using

God's gifts and talents, as parents anointing children with love and care.

But there is a time when we need to respond to God's invitation to rest, to allow for Sabbath time in our lives. Perhaps the time must be short. Perhaps we must create a "gate", just for a day—keeping the Lord's Day holy.

Then the Mondays of our lives will find the crowds pressing on us once more. And once more we must do as Jesus taught and feed them ourselves.

7500

Joseph's Black Coat

The Grey Nuns of the Sacred Heart! A new congregation! A child of the Sisters of Ottawa, Canada, birthed in Buffalo New York! It was 1921. A year later, the congregation accepted an invitation to settle on a stretch of property in Melrose Park, Pa.

There, the charism of Marguerite our founder and Saint came alive at 7500 West Avenue. It would fill the spacious property with a Motherhouse, grade school, high school, day school, gymnasium and residence. Here it would thrive for over 60 years.

The residence was filled with Grey Nuns serving in those schools and even in other schools in the diocese. At a point in that history I found myself in that house of 40 sisters and teaching at the on campus high school.

A house of that size required each of us to take on the multiple housekeeping tasks. Thus, for a time, I became the sacristan. Sacristans were responsible for all that concerned the care of the chapel and Mass. I seemed to be doing fine and enjoyed this responsibility.

Yet, there occurred a time when the whispered buzz was that the plants on the altar were not fresh, ill cared for. I guess I was surprised a bit that sisters did not appreciate the branches without the blooms.

Then the opportunity for revenge arose. One who was a "buzzer" had returned from a late ministry meeting, had paused to pray in the chapel and left, leaving her coat in one of the pews. Disorderly, I thought.

I took the black coat and placed it over the shoulders of St. Joseph who stood near the altar. It wasn't the multicolored coat proclaimed in scripture, plays and song. But Joseph and his new black coat became my silent, personal buzz.

The sister returned to the chapel. I peeked in and she seemed oblivious of Joseph's new garment. A chuckling companion took her turn at a peek. Still no recognition! Disappointing! The next morning I hoped to see the newly robed Joseph and a reaction. The coat was there late the night before but morning came and the coat was gone. When had the owner of the black coat realized her loss? When or what had prompted her back to the chapel seeking it? When had she disrobed Joseph of his new black coat?

Many of us have come in touch with the play "Joseph's Multi-colored Coat" and the story of Jacob's gift to his son—a special garment showing favor and possible future leadership. Rather than kill Joseph, his jealous brothers sold him for 20 pieces of silver.

Does that remind you of another story? Remember Jesus' baptism and God's words, "This is my beloved son in whom I am well pleased"! Like the young Joseph whose father favored him and who rose to leadership, this favorite Son was destined by the Father to be the leader, the long awaited Messiah. Yet, there were priestly leaders who were jealous of his arrival and his looking like a King greeted by waves of palm branches as he entered Jerusalem.

The plotting began. What was the motive of this "brother" of Jesus—Judas, his companion? Did Judas accept the 30 pieces of silver realizing it was to end in more than Jesus' arrest?

Jesus' new robe—purple, a sign of his being regal! After the mockery, he was stripped of that purple and dressed in his own clothes—a seamless white tunic, one that bore the blood of his scourging, not one "dipped in goat's blood" as was Joseph's, a false indicator of his being dead. Later Jesus' executioners would gamble for that garment.

Unlike the young Joseph, Jesus' multicolor coat was actually two garments—one colored to mock and the other his own innocent white. But Joseph in the chapel wore only one—a black coat—the sign of a coat that had been worn by an exhausted nun as she was saying good night to God, to Mary and perhaps Joseph after her long day in ministry.

Think about it . . .

and enjoy the musing

Did the pray-ers actually see Moses and Elijah?

4 The Front Porch

4

The Front Porch

The front porch was not unique to our Riverside house. One might walk down most streets in the neighborhood and notice that each side of the street was lined with front porches. This architectural phenomenon spoke of the style of life enjoyed in those days.

"Those days"—the days when I was growing up were days when front doors were closed but not locked, when backyard fences predated tweeting, when milk was left near the back door, when the clothes line revealed something about the people indoors.

In those days a front porch was another room—one located outside the house and frequently spilling occupants of the house on to this outdoor place. The front porch had a life of its own. It was decorated with outdoor chairs, gliders or rockers. It was like a playroom for either adults or children depending on the time of day. For privacy or protection from rain or sun there were awnings—shades that might be rolled up or down at will.

I remember our front porch, the <u>fourth</u> house on the right on a one way street. It was there that we welcomed many a visitor who came invited or a passing neighbor who stopped to chat a bit, where news good or bad was proclaimed. It was a kind of café where dad would strum his guitar, mom her harmonica and friends would sing between sips of beer. For kids the porch was sometimes an oversized, walk in doll house. For older kids it was a place to just hang out or guzzle a five cent, eight ounce, bottle of pop.

And I remember Art, games of chess and the railing on our front porch. I had learned the game of chess at seventeen, while working as a substitute playground supervisor. Each neighborhood seemed to enjoy its favorite activity. Maybe it was dart games, checkers . . . whatever. I was always invited to participate. One such park activity was chess. This was a new experience for me. I knew nothing of the game. But as the summer moved along my interest was peeked although I lost games to all the twelve year olds as they taught me the game.

Armed with a new chess set, and with no talent, I dared to invite my fiend Art to be my competition. So it was that we frequently straddled the front porch railing—our makeshift table—for a game of chess. Art always left the porch with a final word—"checkmate". But the front porch, and its railing, long remained a place where two teens simply found a time to be chess-mates.

Picture those days when Jesus was a boy in Nazareth. Homes were simple shelters. Doors opened into spaces that we might call a kitchen or a place to cook and sit to eat, a bedroom area or areas and not much more. Doors opened out to an open space where much of the household activities or chores or visiting were done—on the outside, in the open, in public. There, where there were no front porches!

The boy Jesus, like his family and all his Nazarene neighbors, spent a good deal of his time, at play, at chores, with friends, in the outdoors. It was a common meeting place. Scripture offers no particulars but anthropology shares this picture of living in those days.

The man Jesus, having grown up without what we call a front porch was familiar with his own "front porch". It was an outdoor "porch" provided by nature and providing him with a venue for speaking to people. Scripture suggests that he might be invited into others' homes as he was passing by. And, it reveals something about that outdoor "porch" as it breaks open the stories—stories about speaking to people on a hillside or near the seashore or on a mount.

In those days it was common for gatherings to be held in outdoor settings, for preachers to offer their message as they were passing by. Theirs was a message inviting people to pause, to come and listen. John the Baptist appeared in the desert and near the Jordan River proclaiming a message of repentance—an invitation to those who were passing by his "front porch".

Jesus went into towns and on the Sabbath he preached in their synagogues. Yet, Scripture also describes him passing through a field of grain, walking along the Sea of Galilee all the while sharing his message. Often the messages and parables were borrowed from the very elements of nature. It describes the many times when people met Jesus on his "porch" and, listening to him, sought his healing touch or invited him into their homes where healing was needed.

There is something about the front porch, about nature's front porch, that generates a spirit of openness, trust, and a revelation of truth. In those days, it was from within that venue that people would hear the invitation to salvation. Nature's porch. It was a porch built in the very beginning, in those days when the Father first pronounced a creative word and called it . . . "Good".

Even today as I slip open the glass door and step onto my 12th floor patio-porch, I see God's hand in the flowing Niagara River to my right. And ahead, in the gray stone building, I know an older Art is somewhere there . . . playing chess?

9

"Sanctam Esse"

The story began in 1770 and burst into the 20th century, to 1990, when Rome welcomed pilgrims wearing blue scarves and celebrating the canonization of their founding mother, Marguerite d'Youville. The following reflection was printed in the BLFOJournal Vol.1 No.2 when Marek, a former student on that staff, invited me to capture the canonization for the journal. So, I wrote:

French, English, Italian, Latin, Greek, Spanish, Japanese, Portuguese—the idiom of the People of God raised in celebration to the name Marie Marguerite d'Youville, "saint." What belonged to the Grey Nuns so personally as a life model, the revered foundress whose life witness has been emulated by thousands of women since she, and three companions who shared her love and concern for the poor, consecrated themselves to God and promised to serve him in the person of the poor, now seemed to be taken out of the cloister of her spiritual family into the embrace of the Church Universal.

No longer does Marguerite—Mother d'Youville—belong only to the generations of women persevering in her spirit of universal charity, always opening their hands to the needy, willing to be counter-cultural in order to make the gospel a lived reality.

Now Marguerite d'Youville, the 18th century widow, elevated to sainthood by the 20th century Church, stands with a litany of men and women of the ages recognized by the heroic virtue of their lives.

But, Mother d'Youville herself, anonymous as she moved and worked among the poor of her day, was less the hero and more the object of derision. Only time turned her first title "soeurs grises" from the derogatory "tipsy nuns" to its affectionate "grey nuns". and this time, December 9th, 1990, offered her the title "saint".

Here in Rome, motherhouse of the Church, far from her Montreal origins, Marguerite d'Youville's life on earth is declared holy and all are invited to a communion with her. Here in Rome, the city of time and the timeless, 1737 and 1990 now yields to the endless ages of such a communion . . . Here in Rome, in the language of the Church, the Holy Father solemnly pronounces in the name of the Holy Trinity and in the memory of the Apostles Peter and Paul: ". . . *Beatam Mariam Margaritam d'Youville Sanctam esse . . .*" The assembly responds in song, *"Amen. Alleluia."*

Amen. Alleluia. Blue scarves, waved by the two thousand Grey Nuns and friends of Marguerite d'Youville each chanting his or her own Amen. Alleluia . . . and among all, I too waved my scarf and chanted Amen. Alleluia.

Saint Marguerite d'Youville! Did this valiant woman need to be canonized? Does it make a difference that her holy life now be so proclaimed and that this assurance be offered that she has attained a place in heaven? This action, delicately placed in the context of the Mass—the Church's extreme expression of continuity with Jesus Christ—reminds all believers that faith and love must overflow into a life of serving compassion.

To Grey Nuns, striving to be true to the mission of their founding mother, canonization marked a celebrated moment of authenticity, of unity with Marguerite and each other. Yet the compelling call of universality prevailed. Twenty Grey Nuns from Buffalo (and others from our U.S. congregation) shared this event with Grey Nuns from Canada, Japan, Brazil, South Africa, the North Pole and other parts of the world.

To those who accompanied the Grey Nuns to Rome, who have shared other journeys with them—as professional colleagues, as family, as graduates of their schools, as people who have benefitted from the outreach of Grey Nun activity—it was a celebrated moment of relationship. Native Americans were there. And, Lise Normand was there too.

To Lise Normand, the moment of canonization must have held its own interior joy and relationship. Lise participated in the celebration and moved modestly among the 2,000 pilgrims. But it was Lise who offered the living testimony that public veneration and intercession belong to those called "saint."

The power of Marguerite's intercession before God was clearly evidenced when Lise, stricken with myeloblastic leukemia—an incurable disease—was miraculously cured in three weeks after her family and friends began praying to Marguerite. Ten years later, Canadian medical specialists recognized that the cure was permanent and certified that it was "beyond an ordinary cure." This great favor opened for Marguerite the door to the official proclamation of sainthood. And, the tapestry of Marguerite d'Youville, standing with the poor, hung over the door of St. Peter's in Rome, signaled that something special was happening here. That something special was celebrated in ritual and relationship by the pilgrims who came wearing a simple blue scarf.

Now the Grey Nuns and the Church surrender Saint Marguerite d'Youville to all who seek God and find him in the testimony of neighbor loving neighbor.

"Any Friend of God's is a Friend of Mine" (1996, Basilica Press) writes the author, Patrick Madrid. Among the biblical references he offers for intercessory prayer is from Paul's letter to the Romans 15: 30-32: *I urge you brothers by our Lord Jesus Christ and by the love of the Spirit, to join me in the struggle by your prayers to God on my behalf.* He calls these "mini-mediators." The book offers a biblical and historical explanation of the Catholic doctrine of the Communion of Saints.

We recall how Jesus offered Mary to us not only as saint, full of grace, but as mother—"behold they mother". Many times I have lifted up a picture of my mom—my mini-mediator—and whispered a prayer of loving memory, of seeking her guidance or assistance, knowing that she is a step nearer to my God than I.

Remember the wedding at Cana? It was the place and event where Jesus opened his ministry with a miracle. Yet, although Jesus was present, the host approached Mary with his need. Mary, a woman at that! Hadn't Mary immediately turned to Jesus with his concern?

They say "through Mary to Jesus." I add "through St. Marguerite d'Youville to Jesus."

On that 9th day of December, as I personally experienced the canonization event, no book was needed to convince me of our communion—saints on earth with saints in heaven—more than the faith of Lise Normand as she paused for a picture with me on the steps of the Vatican.

12

In the Habit

The hue and cry of student actors at Melrose High School was "we want to do 'The Trouble with Angels!" Well, I had trouble finding the play script for it.

Finally, a graduate presented me with "Life with Mother Superior", the book from which the movie evolved. I remember the small blue hard covered book. It was a very short book. Writers of the movie script must have really put on their creative hats to let the story emerge from those few pages.

As was my custom when obstacles impeded my plans, I turned to a possible plan 'B'. I rented the movie and taped the sound track. I selected the scenes I wanted to use. Donna, one of my dedicated actors during her four years at Melrose, hand copied the dialogue from the selections I made. Her tedious effort offered me what I needed to create our version of "The Trouble with Angels".

The sisters in the movie story were an unidentified congregation of nuns, a kind of traditional image. My plan was to get the twelve student-nun players in the habit of my congregation, the Grey Nuns. Thus, I made an appeal and two Grey Nuns volunteered to help. Since our sisters were no longer wearing the habit, none was available to borrow. The two—Sisters Therese and Mary Sue—ventured into a fabric store and came away with material for their task, a whole lot of ingenuity and a long labor of love. The end was a decent, simpler replica of the original Grey Nun habit for each of twelve students. Perfect especially from a distance!

Students observing the play rehearsals with the nun scenes fell into silence as the twelve sisters walked into the chapel, hands folded, chanting the "Glory Be" in Latin. It was the quietest time during rehearsals and on lookers lamented that they had not signed up to be a nun.

They wanted to be a nun! Well, in the play of course! Yet, I found that an interesting response. The main character of the movie was fascinated by the Mother Superior and at the end of the story entered the congregation.

I look back and wonder then, why none of the lamenters entered the Grey Nun congregation after graduation. The habit? It was most likely being in the habit that was their fascination and not a life call.

Today we may look around and be in touch with sisters. And look one must since the habit is not the necessary garb of many sisters today, nor was it when twelve student players chanted their role across the Melrose stage.

Pope John XXIII had called a council that intended to change the role of the Church by opening its windows and allowing the freshness of the Spirit to enter. It was Vatican II and that council that invited sisters to follow the charism of their founders and their real habits were to be the visible sign of discipleship marked by serving the people of God.

Mary comes to my mind. Mary was not an angel but a teen aged girl. She was not away in a private Catholic school. Rather, I picture her alone, perhaps near her bed preparing to sleep. She is greatly troubled when an angel appears to her with a strange greeting. What is this message?

Is this the role she, a virgin espoused to Joseph, had anticipated? To be a mother? To be the mother of the Son of God? God's mother? What would she wear as she walked onto the stage of motherhood?

I look at the young girl in the scene once more. She is clothed with innocence and accepts the overshadowing of the Holy Spirit. Her life garment, her habit, as it were, is "Grace".

Mary becomes not simply the mother of Jesus. This is the mother of the awaited Messiah, the mother of God. She wears those titles under a more recognizable or visible "mother of sorrows". Even grace does not promise her freedom from sorrow. It is the habit she is called to endure as she walks along the life road with her Son—during their flight from Herod's infanticide, listening to the promise made her at Jesus' presentation and when standing helpless at the foot of the cross.

Likely neither you nor I have been troubled by angels. Rather we are God's children who have been offered grace, the ultimate gift of God's presence within us. It is what urges us to respond to a personal life call. There is a time for us to say "yes" and accept the stirrings of the Holy Spirit as we walk along, wearing a habit or not, chanting our prayer in the vernacular—Glory be to the Father, to the Son and to the Holy Spirit.

23
"Ethni-City"

"Ethni-City" is a word that describes ECC City. It is a college campus, a place that is marked by the variety of "ethnics" who enter its doors, who walk side by side in its halls. They are both students and faculty. They may be Polish or Russian; Liberian or Nigerian; South African or Puerto Rican; Catholic, Protestant or Evangelical; Atheist or Agnostic; White, Black, Yellow or any mixture of races. For them ethnicity means belonging to ECC City, being "City".

Sue Thomas' comments*** about "The Big Fat Greek Wedding" rose from her article and reminded me of what makes ECC City such a rich place. The faculty, staff and students take pride in being Ethni-City. They care about each other and enjoy being on this City site of the college. Being City for them "is a self-reflecting pair of glasses through which we see ourselves and relate to each other . . . a self reflecting lens through which we understand ourselves and interpret our world".

Thomas' remarks were offered in the context of a celebration of a wedding. For Campus Ministry and Ethni-City folks, our celebration was not a wedding but a laureate.

A Senior Laureate! The name was borrowed from the Olympic Games where the laurel was placed on the head of each event winner who represented a particular ethnic group. In our Ethni-City at the college our lens is one of understanding

---

** (used: with permission: Sue Thomas: Everyday Catholic, May 2006, St. Anthony Messenger)

ourselves, interpreting our world and seeing that who senior students have become is worthy of honor.

For over twenty years, Campus Ministry paused to proclaim the achievements of each graduating class—to honor Ethni-City seniors with our symbolic laurels—personal recognition, gifts to each, a gathering of faculty, family and friends to celebrate their educational triumphs. The celebration was followed by a meal where those gathered might say "so long now and thanks for the journey".

The years of celebration passed—1986-2007! Campus Ministry's door closed. Would there be continuity? The yes came where the two roads diverged. And they—a professor and Matthew (former president of the CMA)—they took the one less traveled, one of leading the Campus Ministry Student Association into a year's road through 2007-2008 and toward a final Senior Laureate.

Their theme "The Road Less Traveled" had become a lived experience for them. May 17th arrived and from along this less traveled road they offered laurels at the 23rd and last Senior Laureate . . . . and that has made all the difference for Ethni-City class of 2008 and for the two people who will long share a memory . . .

I shall be telling this with a sigh . . .
Somewhere ages and ages hence:

two roads diverged in a wood, and I—
I took the one less traveled by,
and that has made all the difference (Robert Frost)

Jesus made a final journey into Jerusalem. His entry was a prominent one, choosing to enter seated on an ass's colt and people waving palm branches and greeting him with Hosannas.

He had traveled throughout the country without receiving this kingly welcome. And here, the atmosphere was also filled with the whispers of arrest by order of the chief priests and Pharisees.

Yet Jesus took the road into Jerusalem. It was where he would have his last supper with his disciples. He chose the road to his hour, to his betrayal, his arrest and his cross.

In many other places Jesus, who had no where to lay his head, had met people and their physical or spiritual needs—a Samaritan woman, a beggar born blind, a rich young man, Nicodemus, ten lepers, a crippled woman, an officials' dying son, a friend who had died.

There was a certain ethnicity in their description. He celebrated them: men, women, rich, poor, children, adults. There was spiritual healing and teaching, raising the dead, curing the disabled.

But Jerusalem! The people met him in celebration because they had heard good things about him. The leaders heard too and were disturbed by his coming. There was celebration here. But unlike his presence at a Cana wedding or the celebration of the Passover with friends, this celebration was marked by scourging and the cross, his head torn by a wreath—symbolic laurels that crowned him for his unrecognized achievements, his gifts offered in three years of public ministry and the eternal promise that extends on roads beyond Jerusalem.

Now, "we shall be telling this with sighs ages and ages hence . . ." Jesus took a road less traveled—to the cross, "and that has made all the difference". (Frost)

30
Wings and Things

The invitation arrived by email. It was from a friend who said she would be in Buffalo on Saturday. How would I like to get together for dinner . . . at the Anchor Bar? I returned a quick yes for this opportunity for a meal of wings at this historic site, the birth-bar of chicken wings . . . and of course a visit with a friend.

As we approached the Anchor Bar, my friend revealed that she hadn't been there since she last lived in Buffalo thirty years ago and her memory appetite was at work. I wondered if her memory also stored some shared postulant moments that dotted our early history—some never to be admitted. They were innocent acts committed in the experience of being, rather hopefully becoming . . . full fledged nuns.

Why was the parking lot filled? Not one space including handicap parking! Then the light—today is Saturday and weekend bar and restaurant folks were converged at one of their favorite places. It didn't help that the Preakness would be running on this evening as well.

We found ourselves seated in the bar area. We had bypassed the list for the more respectable side rooms, and the privacy they provided, for a small table, quickly offered in deference to my using a walker and not being able to stand long waiting for a table. A lucky break at the cost of noise and bar company! Neither of us was familiar with this seating so close to bar and bodies lined in front. And the noise! But the sounds were happy ones and people shuffled politely through the tight aisle space.

We chatted with each other and with the bar group as each passerby nearly touched elbows with us (or the walker in the aisle leaning on our table). What they really touched was the felt experience of sharing an outing with a friend. Some standing at the bar became our waiters although that false realization was not discovered until those "waiters" were leaving.

Our voices were soon absorbed as one with the cheering crowd, eyes focused on the TV above the bar as the Preakness ran the course. We became a part of the bar enthusiasm with our shouts urging the only female horse to win the race. And, she did!

In the midst of an apparent chaotic bar setting we snuck in intimate conversation about our current lives hers in Philly, mine in Buffalo. We were soon interrupted by the arrival of our meal—served by an assumed "bar waiter".

We looked with amazement at what 30 wings looked like next to the rest of our order and forced to occupy every bit of space on our miniature table for two (with no room for elbows). Had we ordered all that? Oh well, we could ask for a takeout container and, with each bite taken at a later time, we could pause and remember all the wings and things we experienced at the Anchor Bar that Saturday night.

On other wing trips at the Anchor Bar, I have been seated in what I might call a respectable setting—in one of the side rooms with the privacy of a table. Being so near the bar was unfamiliar and what I first might have called less than nice company.

I think of the call of Matthew (also named Levi) a tax collector. Jesus simply said "Follow me" and then went to eat at his house. Others joined them for the meal. Scripture names them "many tax collectors and sinners". The other eleven were criticized for participating. No words of repentance are spoken by Matthew—,

Matthew, out of this company of guests, who would enjoy being called to be one of twelve Apostles.

Yet when Jesus invited himself to dinner at the home of Zacchaeus, Luke writes that the twelve were appalled; they grumbled about his going to the house of a sinner. Were there other guests? If so what were their sins? We only know that one was a tax collector. Zacchaeus himself repented immediately and before the dinner at his house. Even after his repentant words Zacchaeus, a new disciple, is not called to Apostleship as was Matthew.

At another table, Jesus sat with the twelve. This too was a meal. Consider this group. How many had grumbled about the company Jesus had kept? How many seated in his presence were yet to sin—to deny Jesus, to hide rather than speak in his defense or stand near his Cross, to mark Jesus for thirty pieces of silver . . . ?

Twelve sinful men, twelve called to be Apostles!

What am I to learn from these stories? Perhaps it is about judgment, about grumbling about the kind of people who might be called "sinners". It may be a message to me, about my own sinfulness and how I might have judged the people in that place where I came to dine. Or it may be about postulants—and how their "sin" might have been judged . . . had the truth been known.

I think it was a reminder that I ought not to have put myself above some named "sinners" as I sat in the midst of the "bar crowd" . . . : at a tiny table near to them and to my wings . . . and, yes, near the "bar waiter" who reached out to serve us.

48

God Is In the City

My eyes fell on the page opened at random to Psalm 48. Its words rose from the page and rested in my discerning heart—"God is in the City".

"God is in the City". The psalmist had no idea that the words would be prophetic in 1982, bearing an invitation, an opening to a 20th century journey and ministry.

The newly named Campus Minister entered an historic reality—the beautiful Romanesque structure housing Erie Community College—City Campus. Recalling the psalmist's words, I offered a "yes". That "yes" became a commitment that would inspire me to keep a spiritual reality alive, the invitation trusting that God is in the City.

Five years ago I had reflected on the journey: "20 years ago . . . I walked into the halls of this architectural charm with its new name and residents. A far cry from the less than charming name "Old Post Office"! It was August 1982. I had prayed about coming here. And, the Psalms had prompted me. That is what lured me to come and that is what I have fixed my eyes on since".

God's presence in this City Campus, that truth, became evident in the many students and faculty who heard his call . . . "come to the water, come without money".

Yes, they came where God's promise led them to be satisfied in their need. Some came hungry, others homeless. They came thirsting for spiritual guidance, consolation in times of grief, to share jubilation and seek reconciliation, to pray and hear God's good news.

Some came bearing their gifts. They came, Jew and Gentile, to participate in recognizing God's presence among them in the community. They became with their willingness to serve together in God's name, in the name of Campus Ministry.

Mary's ministry began with her "yes", not to a psalmist's prompting but from an angel. It was the beginning of her ministry, of bearing the Christ to all . . . to those who were thirsting. Mary would tell her Son, "They have no wine". And through this woman, a minister in time of a need, would He not satisfy the thirsty guests? Campus Ministry was that place offering to satisfy spiritual thirsts but remaining aware that our "guests" could also be refreshed with a good cup of coffee as they journeyed from class to class.

Remember the discouraging words of the travelers on their way to the city to be registered in the census: "There's no room!" How many times would they be denied? Campus Ministry received that message of denial six times. Six times the Ministry found shelter at an atrium at a cafeteria table while waiting in anticipation for an offer of an available room. Yet, even there in that interim open space, students paused and those who sought privacy used a cell phone to contact me in my current open space.

Rooms offered, rooms denied—532, 500, 275, 475, 275 and 532 once more. The last of those rooms, 532, once the first, it was as though the years had begun a new cycle. But an irony marked 532—that this first space would be the last. This denial happened coincidently with a phone call and a different denial, one born in the wake of a diocesan "journey of faith": "I am sorry to tell you we are no longer supporting Campus Ministry at this non-residential college." The end.

God had found shelter in the City for twenty five years. The Campus Minister now closed the door behind her and began a search for another "city".

How many times in Scripture do we read about people looking for their needs to be satisfied! They don't have to search far. It seems that just within sight they arrive where help is. That welcoming space is called "Jesus". And, just as Jesus was present to those who called out "Lord, Lord . . .", Campus Ministry opened its space to similar calls. After all, the response was expected. Yes, expected where ministry provided a presence especially to needs expressed in a college community.

But pause for a moment. Consider how each of us, baptized with Water and the Spirit, has been called to provide the same ministry.

Scripture is firm about that call. It does not speak about Campus Ministry or parish outreach. Instead, we read in Matthew, words like: being separated—goats on the left from sheep on the right, inheriting the kingdom, whatever you did to the least, I was hungry, thirsty, you gave me no welcome . . . Those are words spoken about the last judgment.

That is the moment when each of us must personally stand and from our particular "532" space, be ready to offer an open invitation—"Come, you who are blessed by my Father. Inherit the kingdom for I was hungry and you fed me . . .".

64

Last Stops

What is a last stop? And how many times have we experienced a "last stop"? Memories of "last stops" came to me recently.

Where was I going? I remember the bus driver's voice calling out the next stop: "Kosciusko Street". That was my last stop when visiting my East side cousin usually for an overnight visit. There was another bus ride with the last stop in Buffalo. Six hours from Mahanoy City in Pa. thirteen seventh graders accompanied by their teacher—me, had planned a class trip on their small budget and raffle ticket sales.

Not all last stops are as pleasant. There was the Riverside Park bench which rescued me from an intended visit to my Aunt's house in North Tonawanda. It became my last stop when the wind became too difficult for a teen age biker to contend with. A plunge into Ellicott Creek was my last stop when I had hoped to simply enjoy a canoe ride. The middle of the ski slope at Kissing Bridge was my last stop on the slope. The fall, the failure of my boot to release from the ski, and a broken ankle landed me in a hospital rather than a successful day on the slopes.

After high school, I took a last stop working at Woolworth's rather than following my dream of college and a career. The bump was there and I paused long enough to explore its gifts to me as a person. When the time was right, I hopped over the bump and pushed forward into my dream and the possibilities that lay beyond.

Three teachers from St. Canicus School gathered their classes for the Holy Thursday traditional visit to seven churches. But there were only six catholic churches in town. A large number in a town where the walk would take about twenty minutes to and from! We needed another church. Aha! The chapel in our convent home! It provided a holy visit and some hot chocolate to relieve us from the chill of that spring evening. Our last stop . . . until Good Friday.

Last stops mean we've already been somewhere, that we are coming from where we've been. I think that last stops are where life experiences have introduced a bump in our journey. We hit the bump and stop. Or, we hurdle the bump for the possibilities open to us on the other side. We move on to those other last stops.

Remember "Quo Vadis"? The title of an historical novel and a '50s movie takes place in the time of Nero around 64 AD. Quo Vadis? . . . "Where are you going?"

Quo Vadis: Where are you going?" The question also alludes to the acts of Peter in which Peter flees Rome but on his way meets Jesus and asks him where he's going. When Jesus answers "Where I go you cannot follow me now . . . though you will follow later . . ." the words do not offer him any specific information.

Peter does follow Jesus . . . to Rome. He seems oblivious of the real meaning of "follow me', a kind of bump. His companion disciple had experienced a similar oblivion. Two had reached last stops. There was no bus driver to warn either: only the cock crowing and the non-returnable thirty coins would be omens, would be stumbling blocks. One would overcome his obstacle and the other succumb to his.

Rome would indeed be the place to where Peter would follow Jesus. It was Rome that would be the place of his martyrdom, where he would truly follow Jesus. It would be Peter's last stop.

Jesus had called out an invitation. Or, might one look back and call it a warning—: "you will follow later"?

As if an echo of that call, it became Peter's last stop.

70
Who Is My Neighbor?

God's word often speaks to us at times when we least expect. It is easy to listen to a gospel story and kind of dismiss it with a shrug and thoughts like: "I've heard this one" or "I get it". But the message may linger and reappear in the events of our lives. Then it is important to put on the brakes and recognize what is right in front of you.

Recently, one of those familiar gospels told the story of a Good Samaritan. The priest offered a homily challenging our neighborliness. My mind drifted to the summer of '70.

I had left the convent near the end of my Canonical year. The message that my Mom had suffered a stroke urged my decision to go home, to be with my family during this time of uncertainty about my mom's future.

On an August morning I was returning home after an early morning Mass and looking forward to a first cup of coffee. As I passed the rectory on Chadduck Ave., I noticed a man standing near his car just a few doors away. He was apparently experiencing car trouble. I drove by and with a nonchalant evaluation. I thought—"one of the neighbors will come to his aid." I had not taken into consideration that it was 7:30 am, that perhaps the man was on his way to work, that his neighbors might still be asleep and thus there'd be no response to the immediacy of his need.

When I got to the corner of the block, God called me to stop. I put on the brakes as his words echoed from a very familiar gospel story with a challenge—"Ruth, you are his neighbor".

What could I do? I turned the car around and approached the distressed man and his car. I was able to offer what he needed. It was the need of another car so that he might jump start his own.

It was over that morning coffee that I reflected on the event and how God had chosen the time and place for me to experience being "neighbor".

The recent reading of the gospel of the Good Samaritan had taken me back years to an ordinary event. The homily that followed proposed questions about our attitude, about being a good neighbor . . . today.

We know the story of the man who was beaten and robbed and left by the wayside. A priest and a Levite passed him by supposing someone else might assist him. It was a Samaritan—the least respected of the three who paused to respond to the immediate need of the man and then care for his ongoing needs. Perhaps we like to admit that we'd be the Samaritan.

The homily suggested we check three questions to reveal our attitude about being a good neighbor. It might be good to read the gospel story again with those questions in mind: "What's in it for me"? Or, "Why should I bother"? Or, "What can I do to help"?

The event I remembered was over forty years ago. But in this recent re-telling of the gospel story there is a call from God, even now, to remember and to be ready and open with the best attitude.

We can answer our own question," Who is my neighbor?"

82

"Just Be Present"

When he dropped me off at my convent residence, I remember the words he left me with to ponder: "just be present". My friend Fr. Paul, a seasoned Campus Minister, offered me the single advice that would be behind everything that I would do over the next 25 years.

As I walked down the steps of City Campus in 2007, I was aware of taking my last steps after twenty five years as Campus Minister and I reflected on my first walk up those steps carrying the words of advice in my novice ministry backpack.

It was the summer of '82. I entered the massive Gothic structure covering an entire city block. Dubbed the old post office, it was recently adapted for use as a college. I was greeted by the great sky lighted atrium that dominated the central portion of the building and was surrounded by four floors of arched galleries and pale ecru walls. As I stood there, I felt an upward surge, an enticement to respond to the scriptural invitation of my prayer. The words echoed in the vastness of what I was witnessing. They began:

"Yahweh loves his city founded on the holy mountain . . .
He has glorious predictions to make of you, city of God!"

But, other words—"Just be present". How was that possible when I realized I was a newly named Campus Minister with the burden of scripture that called me to that ministry?

The semester began with the question still looming. Now, as I approached the great Atrium I was overwhelmed by the students filling it and the halls that surrounded it. I had to escape. I hurried to the room assigned for me to use as an office. It was empty, still awaiting the promise of desk and chairs. I sat down on the floor to consider my situation. What to do? "Just be present"! I was not up to a return to the Atrium and unfamiliar faces. Alone! I felt alone. I had become what campus ministry dubs a "lone ranger" minister.

I reached into my bag for paper and a marker. I made several flyers—invitations that I would post on each floor. They simply read:

Anyone interested in Campus Ministry
Join me in Room 530 for Information
Tuesday at 1pm

Twelve students came to that first gathering. They became the nucleus of that first semester—my first semester at the college. Now Fr. Paul's words were in effect as I stepped out of that empty room present to twelve students who were beginning a journey as the Campus Ministry Association. Being present became easier with those early disciples.

First, it was expressed by activities with them. Together we forged a way to reach into the Atrium and be present to campus life and needs. Then coffee became the grounds for being present as students, faculty and staff stepped into the once empty space for a beverage. From those casual meetings and planned events there were opportunities to be present, to enter into the life and needs of the people who made up City Campus.

Thus a first day slipped almost unnoticed into the hundreds of days that add up to 25 years of a lone ranger's "just being present"!

I remember a film I saw called "The Ant Hill". The story begins with the Holy Trinity looking down from heaven on an ant hill below. Things are out of control there. The Father recognizes the need to do something to correct the situation. He decides to send down his Son. As the Son departed, perhaps his Father's words of advice echoed those I heard "Just be present!" And Jesus did. He became an ant.

Jesus became present to us as man. He came with love and to correct the mischief of the two who lived in a garden and allowed weeds to overwhelm them and affect future generations.

Now, in this new persona, more a lone ranger than the expected image of an expected regal Messiah, Jesus goes about being present wearing the garment of man. He invites twelve to assist him as he breaks into his ministry. He meets people in their need and offers them consolation, healing and an invitation to "follow me".

The cost of this ministry was a fidelity to the absolute presence to God's people.

Unlike my simple offer of "coffee", Jesus offered the ultimate signs of his commitment—his own blood spilled, his body nailed to a criminal's cross.

Earlier, he had promised his twelve disciples that he would not leave them. The promise was fulfilled when his thirty three years slipped away in death and resurrection . . . yet remain with us as his Divine Meal and gift of the Holy Spirit.

Jesus' thirty three years add up to over two thousand "just being present"!

400

Julia "Drops-In"

How proficient are you with social media? I feel overwhelmed as a litany of new vocabulary is presented to name the ever growing tools of this media. I am left without a description of each one's major function let alone the multiple aspects and the' how to' of them.

Example! Recently I was introduced to dropbox. Sounds fine! It is intended to exchange documents in a jiffy and much more efficiently, easier than email attachments. After several attempts encouraged by Julia I decided to try to send some documents via this alleged "better way" into a friend's shared dropbox thus connecting two people over 400 miles apart.

Drag and drop, directions flustered my old ways with all the key+ and other commands. I paused . . .

Since I feared the negatives—accidental changes, lost documents and heaven' knows what more—that motivation urged me to slip backwards and do my task the long familiar way—copy, select-paste A compromise for now! Create a whole new file of the documents! Maybe later I might venture into the new and attempt to simply (?) drag and drop!

If I thought opening the directions for using some of the buttons on my microwave—on /off, timer, frozen items, reheat, pop-corn, etc.—was problematic, you can only imagine my dropbox issues.

Thus what was . . . is now operative again. And, what may yet be . . . is a rush to my social media brain center (if there is one at all) of a flood of details that flows into an understandable stream.

The world screams "social media!" and their advances echo the great human capacity, the gift of intellect and reasoning that ushers us forward. However, at my computer it is I who does the screaming.

We lost something when sin filled a dropbox: God-humans with its activity in a garden and the advances into the world—creation of today.

The God of creation had burned into the human a heart with the understanding of right and wrong accompanied by free will—to make the choices intended for us to actually choose the good. Yet, thousands of years later, we are reminded of Moses holding up two stone tablets offering a reminder of what every human being knows in his very being—10 simple rules (Decalogue). Peek into that dropbox! What a reminder they became! A dispersed community of chosen people reverenced the tablets and carried them on their journeys. But too often that reverence was lost when understanding was blurred in favor of the social media—when their social choices caused them to slip away from their God and bow to false gods, sinful behavior and pleasurable choices. A repetitious cycle began—they sinned, they cried out to God for help, and God favored them each time with a renewed covenant relationship. Thus the dropbox was filling up over the centuries.

In another era it was Jesus who spoke to the people. His social media was to offer the crowds a Sermon on the Mount. There were no stone tablets to reach stony hearts here. This Jesus built on the old but advanced it's understanding, God's logo from the beginning, urged the listeners with the Beatitudes—the paths that lead to the Kingdom of Heaven. They confronted the listener with decisive moral choices leading to participation in the divine nature of God.

God's social media fulfill his promises from his act of creation, through Abraham . . . Moses, to the salvific Word made flesh—Jesus. It is God's gratuitous gift begun in the beginning to reach hearts open to the new.

What about us today? Do we open His dropbox to check the "documents" filed there? To recognize the old as alive in the new? After all, Jesus came not to destroy the old but to fulfill it.

And we? Do we find ourselves accepting the old—that which was in our hearts from the beginning—and living it out in the new? When I pray before the Cross and bow before the Blessed Sacrament, I call out: "May the heart of Jesus in the most blessed sacrament be praised, adored and loved in all the tabernacles of the world . . . especially in the tabernacle of my body"!

498

Sitting Alone?

"Why are you sitting alone?" Laura, a multilingual guest posed the question and I realized my answer fell short of what I was experiencing.

Here in Chateauguay, on Isle Saint-Bernard, 498 boul.d'Youville, Manoir d'Youville was founded in 1964 as a hostelry for rest, vacation, retreat or conferences. It emerged out of the history of the Grey Nuns of Montreal and Saint, Marguerite d'Youville.

Paintings and pictures line the walls of the Manoir with reminders of that history and the figure of the woman Marguerite. Her statue is at the entrance of the chapel, hands outstretched in welcome, inviting one into a holy place where the tabernacle is a prominent sign of deep religious faith. Within these walls of the Manoir one is hosted in the welcoming charism of the Grey Nuns by the gracious sisters and staff.

Outside, surrounded by Lac St-Louis, the Island, purchased by then Madame d'Youville, reminds one of the history of her canoe trips between Old Montreal and the island where she came to teach her religion to the children of the area and to serve the needs of the poor.

The apple orchard was there in the mid 1700s. Were there 300 trees then? There was wild life there. But, today the land is graced by 10 km of wildlife refuge paths known as "refuge Marguerite d'Youville".

Was I, a Grey Nun sitting alone? Added to the mystique of this place, my silence allowed me to observe the incarnation of sisters from home in the faces and statures of several sisters and guests:

Sandy, an Associate, was there in the presence of the questioning and humorous Laura. Who could miss Sisters Faith, Jean O. or Mary Denis in the mirror images who sat across the room. From hair style and stature and even step I was able to recognize Annie. The dark haired woman who sat and ate so properly seemed none other than Charlotte. What a likeness! And the tall thin figure with the same remembered particular wave of dark hair must be Barbara, a former GN.

The question was raised in the dining hall: "Why are you sitting alone?" Alone? The chattering of sisters and guests as they gathered for meals surrounded me. Their conversations were in their native French language.

The question broke my reverie. Was I sitting alone in the midst of Canadian Grey Nun history? Was I sitting alone with images of my American Grey Nun Sisters so near me and in the silence of my felt experience?

How inadequate my faint reply "I only speak English".

Jesus went up to the mountain to pray. He took with him Peter, James and John—by themselves. But what happened? Jesus was transfigured before them and Moses and Elijah appeared. Jesus was speaking with them.

His fellow pray-ers recognized the faith figures from their Jewish past. They now seemed not alone with Jesus who had led them up the mountain . . . by themselves.

Then while Jesus was still speaking about making tents for each, a cloud overshadowed them and a voice proclaimed identity with Jesus—called him son and said he was pleased with him.

The reaction of the disciples indicates they heard the voice because they fell down and covered their faces for fear. Jesus touched them and when the disciples raised their eyes expecting to see those other figures . . . they saw no one.

Did the pray-ers actually see Moses and Elijah, or hear the conversation, as they appeared and spoke with Jesus? Or were they caught up in the history of their faith?

How often do we share the experience of sitting alone but enjoying the faces of others—memories of faces that emerge on our mountains where we think ourselves alone. They are reminders of the people that accompany us to other places where someone might ask: "Why are you here alone?"

532
The "Lesser"

The concept rose in my current study of philosophy—subsidiarity. Simply, it said the greater ought not do what the lesser can do. It is a concept that flows from being a philosophical principle into application in politics and even into our daily activities.

In an effort to share this important principle with my work study, Jenn, I was suddenly overtaken by her prompt response and application of this tidbit of scholarship. I was thinking to offer her the principle and she immediately attached its evidence to our working relationship—campus minister and student assistant. In a blink we were re-aligned from teacher and student to "greater" and "lesser" by the "lesser".

This application readily turned on me, the greater. While we laughed at the new hats we wore, it became obvious that some changes were in order. I don't know about you but I tend to decide how I want a task accomplished and then pass it on to the one who will perform the task. Now Jenn made me acutely aware that she, the lesser, could perform many tasks without the necessary performance plan. Indeed she not only could, but—ought!

Of course the greater wanted to have her plans executed. Of course she may have translated greater as better and expressed or interpreted them as "my way". Then the lesser, quietly obedient, may have thought about her capability to perform without such specific direction. Interrupting both was, at least, the principle itself

Thus the newly shared principle became one that created a different atmosphere in Room 532, the small office space allotted to Campus Ministry. Perhaps neither Jenn nor I donned our new hats with stubborn adherence but our understanding of the principle was not only the subject of motivation but it became the object of shared humor. And yes, each one's individual growth and a growing relationship!

When I browse through scripture, I recognize times when the "lesser" seems to be God's, the Greater's chosen way, when the "lesser" was called to carry out God's plan of salvation.

We think of the Hebrews who were the lesser, the dominated peoples, slaves to the great and powerful Egypt . . . that the prophet chose David the youngest son from whose family the savior would be born . . . that It was a young and small David who defeated the giant Philippi an.

We celebrate Mary, a teen aged girl, chosen to give birth to the One whom she proclaims "Who am I that my savior would come to me?" and "He who is mighty has done great things to me."

Finally, it is Jesus, the Logo of creation, who accepted the human condition, took on the form of the creature—the one who was created even a little less than the angels.

God's plan took many turns, moved in many directions to achieve the ultimate goal—the covenants with the "lessers", the way of the cross and the salvation of His people.

Through those relationships with the lessers God has given us the opportunity of an eternal relationship with Him, the Greater. We live in the atmosphere of that subsidiary called to carry on the mission entrusted to us . . . the lesser.

Buffalo—Alive and Well Today!

I urge you to discover our City born in 1789 . . . alive and well today—and recently dubbed with its current logo: "Buffalo For Real." At the same time, I remind readers, tourists and all of us that we are still the "City of Good Neighbors"!

A student offered his article for me to read and share (editions noted [ ] by me). Because of the "slam Buffalo opening comments" I was irritated but he urged me to read on . . . and I extend the same invitation. It is my Buffalo, and yes—the real Buffalo.

The Article:

Buffalo, you wouldn't catch me there, it's freezing, all it does is snow, and it's dirty, the summers are boring and nothing ever goes on there. It's not my kind of town."

Wait a minute, you pessimist. I've got some news for you. The City of Buffalo and surrounding areas are brimming with entertainment from the cold winter days to the hot summer nights.

This is one of the most entertaining cities in America. Buffalo's not that dirty frozen block of ice that people are led to believe. This is a town with a cornucopia of power packed activities and a wonderful, positive use of each of the four seasons. I'd like the chance for those misguided souls to be here right now with their erasers, so they can rub out the negative thoughts they probably heard from someone, who heard it from someone else, and so on.

Living here for (48) years, I have heard and read so many negative things about my city, it has gotten to the point that it is sometimes amusing to hear the put downs. Even as I sit quietly writing this by the shores of Lake Erie, I feel the cool spring breeze coming off of it. Adding some color to my scenic pleasure is a great ship gliding effortlessly down the canal on its way to somewhere. It is almost like a page out of Samuel Clemens' book "Huckleberry Finn".

<u>Winter</u>. Yeah, we get winters, and like some other cities it's cold and snowy, but what are you going to do, lock yourself up in your house? Winters are fun if you utilize them right. People actually travel up from the south to ski and hunt here. Buffalo and the surrounding areas have quite the reputation of having some of the best skiing in the country. I've been to a couple of the resorts around here and have found them to have a four star rating. As far as hunting, whitetail deer are plentiful.

<u>Summer</u>. Buffalo summers are the best you can find anywhere in the northeast. Here is a great deal of anticipation for their arrivals. When they do get here, watch out! This city blooms. It always brings on great wonder to me as I watch summer unfold in front of my eyes. Flourishing trees and beautiful flowers are just a little part of nature coming back to life and with it a refreshing and new feeling. Anyone lucky enough to be here for the change of season will attest to this. Buffalo surely knows how its arrival with a huge number of events and gatherings that last through the summer. And, I'll tell you my friend, these bashes are second to none.

Buffalo is the starting and finishing point for many shipping tasks. It has been for over a hundred years *[note our marinas and a popular Marina Park downtown with opportunities to go aboard a real ship docked there or on other visiting ships]*.

Buffalo has quite a selection of entertainment offerings in the summer months, and most are free or very affordable and many in or near your own "backyard". As gas prices skyrocket, you'll be pleased to know that some are only a short drive away. With such a variety of entertainment, I am sure even the toughest critic can be pleased.

Do you like music? There are concerts offered in different locales and times and kinds in the city and nearby as well. In Lewiston, just outside Buffalo, we have Art Park—a full multi-cultural entertainment center that offers a dynamic lineup of free concerts on select evenings with heavier hitter artists such as The Glenn Miller Orchestra, the band "Blood, Sweat & Tears and various blues artists. With different ages of music represented throughout the summer, you're sure to find something to suit your taste.

Art Park also offers arts and crafts and theatre, for the whole family, so you can plan to spend the day.

Closer to Buffalo are the Tonawandas' Gateway Park. This fully renovated facility is situated on the mouth of the historic Erie Canal. It offers a mix of history, beauty and music. The result: another reinforcing reason why you should be thankful you're in Buffalo. It is wonderful that our contributing neighbors can offer free music. That's what I call getting an affordable earful as well as an enjoyable view.

Right here in Buffalo, music lovers can enjoy a Sunday summer afternoon without even reaching into their pockets. Our city proves that we offer all tastes and styles of music by offering live jazz concerts on the steps of the Albright Knox Art Gallery, revered as one of the most popular galleries in the world. In my opinion "art never sounded so good". (Yes, the gallery itself provides an all season offering]. You have to admit there is a double hitter right there! How many home runs do we have so far? [and what about our teams throughout the seasons . . . baseball, basketball, football . . . college and pro offerings!] I have lost count.

I could sit here and offer numerous other entertainment examples offered through Buffalo's lively and colorful seasons, but there are too many. To be honest with you, I would rather you see them for yourself! Music and plays already mentioned [The Sheas, Irish Theatre, The Kavinoky . . . and more], fairs [garden walks], carnivals, [festivals:[, and how about the Eden Corn Festival? renowned Allentown Art festival . . . myriad home food experiences—wings, roast beef on weck . . . and those little *[and popular]* ice cream shops down the street *[Antoinette's . . . sponge candy anyone? Anderson's . . .]*

The fullness we experience in our city with the changing seasons and how we make the best of them makes us strong *[versatile]* and receptive to the joys that have been bestowed upon us here.

This city—Buffalo—opens wide its arms, all year, every year, and wide enough to take you in with hospitality and a richness that, possibly, you have never felt in another city. Hopefully, I can speak for all of us *[Buffalonians]* when I say, "Come to us. Let us embrace you". After you have spent some time here, you may find it painlessly acceptable to change your way of thinking toward us and surprisingly *[admit]*, "Buffalo, I've been here, it is fantastic! The people are warm and the seasons beautiful . . . I cannot wait to come back!"

"What's in a name?" the poet asked. Proverbs responds: *The name of the Lord is a strong tower; the righteous runs into it and is safe.* (Proverbs 18:10)

The Jews of biblical times believed that knowing a person's name was to know the person. A name represented the person—his character, his attributes, his very nature. The name "God" was so full and meaningful that one might only whisper the sounds without the vowels.

In the fullness of time God gave the world a Son and a Name. Scripture recalls the angelic visit to Mary and the words: *Behold, you will conceive in your womb and bear a son, and you shall name him Jesus.*

"Jesus"! Jesus was both proclaimed and disdained. We recall his birth and the proclamations that welcomed him and recognized his kingship. People flocked into his presence to hear his teaching and witness his miracles. But there were whispers denouncing him, false charges and accusations that he was inciting revolt.

Today we cry out and proclaim the name of God's Son—Jesus-. We recognize what he offers: he stretched out his arms on the cross in order to embrace us all and to offer us his welcome—eternal life . . . salvation.

Buffalo has too often been a name whispered by others offering a dire description of this city on the lake. But, a visit here and visitors will experience our Buffalo and proclaim its many great gifts

So . . . "Run in"!

1982

A Return to Eden

Unexpectedly while at prayer I mused over Eden, that place where I had served as principal of a small catholic school. I left there quietly in 1981after three years.

I had toiled there in behalf of the students mindful of the best educational programs we might offer. And that did happen. Our students were often recognized for performing as well and better than their counterparts in the public school. Our teachers were dedicated sisters and laywomen.

Yet in this very garden of education, I missed the growing and subtle infiltration of disgruntled feelings among a few. I had left my guard down allowing the few to take hold of the situation and bring down my tenure there. Oh, I had provided a "guard"—new security at the entrance doors and the speaker contact between office and classrooms—guarded doors and classrooms but missed the subtle breakdown.

In one way I left with my head high for my efforts there and with the support of many. On the other hand, I walked away with a wound. How would I ever return to Eden? The opportunity to return came soon. It was a celebration. I pushed myself and returned for the event. At the sign of peace during the Mass, I turned and faced the instigator of my leaving. My offer of "peace" was sincere and it washed the wound I had left with.

I was welcomed back to Eden a short time later. Eden was inviting me to offer spiritual teaching and leadership to their children preparing for Confirmation. What greater welcoming gift might they have offered me! Now I was entrusted to share in the life giving education of their youth.

What had I learned from this experience in Eden? I suppose it was that the call to serve, to toil, may be disrupted but peace and forgiveness can lead us back.

What happened in the Eden of Genesis? Scripture recounts the task of the first man and woman—to toil and to guard the garden. They were called stewards of the garden. For me, the whole notion of caring seemed to be in the message. Yet, until recently, I had missed an aspect of that caring: "Toil and guard!" My focus had not included "guard".

"Guard!" That would mean there was something to watch out for, to protect against. But I was not alone. Our first occupants of Eden seemed not to have kept their guard. Was it because God had never mentioned that there was someone lurking in their midst? That it was someone demonic, someone who had already taken sides against God? And in that place that presence must not have appeared as dangerous. Else Eve's guard would have been up and Adam would have been more aware. How easily they were deceived. Their guard was down in the subtlety of the situation.

Yes, subtlety. Our parents slipped into a hidden agenda that would ultimately be their downfall. And we are aware of the result. They were expelled from Eden. Yet, the notion of a future return was kind of built in when God promised that a woman would crush the head of the perpetrator. The gift of Eden with its promise would allow for a return even to those who had been expelled.

All of us, children of Adam and Eve, live in the ultimate promise . . . when God's Son would pronounce forgiveness as he looked upon those who had crucified Him. "Father, forgive them . . ."

We thank God for the opportunity to return to our Edens!

2006

A Spin on "Peanut" Ants

The movie is called "The Ant Bully". As I mulled over the thoughts presented by the story, I was soon spinning over to the first Sunday of October and the traditional National Pro-Life Chain. That day finds me and a group of Grey Nun Associates prayerfully standing for "life".

In the 2006 movie, Lucas is a ten year old who is bullied by a neighborhood kid. His sister, parents and aunt are doing their own zany things and Lucas finds that his life is miserable. So the boy looks for someone he can push around and he finds a colony of ants in his backyard. He hates ants. So, he takes out his frustrations by stomping, killing, burying the critters. The ants retaliate. A wizard ant shrinks Lucas to the size of an ant and he is put on trial before the leader of the ant council. He is guilty and his punishment is to live among the ants and discover the difficulty of ant life. A "peanut" of an ant, Lucas is bullied by other ants but later joins them in an all-out successful battle against a pest-control man brought in to get rid of the bugs.

Here's where my spin takes life . . . (Oops, pardon the pun "life").

Abortion is about bullying the peanut baby dubbed "fetus". It's about victimizing by those who simply can. The world of the bully is a primitive one: "where it's every man [woman] for himself [herself]". One of the final comments in the story comes from the ant Head of Council—"To attack without provocation, without reason, just because they can—it's barbaric." Roe vs. Wade arrived as the "pest control man". Get rid of the unwanted critters. The act itself is barbaric.

Yes some might conjure up a reason to attack "peanut" babies. Mindful that reason is not the same as one's opinion, want, choice, it behooves everyone to find a context. I suggest that we heed the Head of our Council—God! "I knew you in your mother's womb . . . I love you and have called you by name".

Yet as we stand along Niagara Falls Boulevard to quietly pray and hold the banners proclaiming "No to Abortion, yes to life", there is a silent bullying that goes on as well. What is known as "the finger" sends its message, its emotional, unreasoned, response from passing cars. And somewhere else—in a Main Street clinic or in clinics in Kansas or other states, the pest control man wears a doctor's white and attacks not only fetuses but late term babies. The barbarous act happens on a table near a doctor's oath:

Most especially must I tread with care in matters of life and death. If it is given me to save a life, all thanks. But it may also be within my power to take a life; this awesome responsibility must be faced with great humbleness and awareness of my own frailty. Above all, I must not play at God.

"Above all, I must not play at God." Yet, this modern version of the oath (1964) is far from the original oath. Who but God is the author of life and death? What ethic? What loyalty to God's plan for humanity? What cultural phenomenon would cry for such a permissible and barbaric action against the child in a mother's womb . . . and even outside the womb? What inspiration would put aside an earlier physician's oath (1948)?:

> I will not give a lethal drug even when asked nor will I advise such a plan and similarly, I will not give a woman a pessary to cause an abortion.

What changes in law, in respect for the human condition would put aside the physician's original Hippocratic Oath?

> I will maintain the utmost respect for human life from the time of conception, even under threat, I will not use my medical knowledge contrary to the laws of humanity.

We must pray. We must silently lift the posters with messages of life. But more, we must rid the root of immoral choices and the persons who carry signs that proclaim "Choice".

In the movie, Lucas is sent to the ant colony by a wizard ant. In Scripture we read that Jesus, is sent by God the Father to live in the human colony. It is in their particular milieus that Lucas and Jesus are both confronted by bullies.

We can imagine the angelic visit to the young girl Mary. Mary's yes sparked the action of the Holy Spirit and she was with child. Bullying would follow because she was not yet with her husband when the child Jesus was conceived. Joseph, her espoused, prevented the bullying that began by taking her into his home as his wife.

This was a time in history when people were waiting for the Messiah and seemed to be most attentive to signs of his coming. Yet, the responses to the events, to what was happening in their midst, were lost in the observances of the law.

As we follow the story of the child we become aware of angels and shepherds who greet the newborn. Life is praised. Then Magi come. Unlike those along the curbs of the Boulevard silently holding posters, they journey along a path bearing gifts, proclaiming a kingly life. But they are silent before the Roman leaders whose jealous pest control rage will be spent on a barbaric response—killing all children under age two. Their oath is to man and not to God. They search relentlessly for this child, a would-be king.

Jesus is spared this extreme bullying when Joseph has a dream that speaks of danger to the child and so he flees to Egypt to protect Jesus' life from the pest controllers.

Observances of the law! What is the right law? Whose law stands as the ultimate one? Roe vs. Wade?! The martyrdom of babies! The old law is repeated Even the child Jesus had to avoid the consequences of a law that devalued life.

Like Lucas, Jesus and his companions present the new law. And, no matter the bullies, both the Lucas story and the Jesus story have this common end—their efforts, their companions, rise to "save their colonies from annihilation".

2011

A True Act of Service

Outside the air created a chill factor of about 13 degrees. Inside, as a group of Grey Nun Associates gathered, the room was warm and comfortable. The only chill was from the feeling of the deep sharing that was being voiced among us.

Joyce led us into that period of sharing by asking us to choose a characteristic of St. Marguerite that we wish to consider for our spiritual growth, a new beginning for the New Year.

It was Chris who spoke first. Her choice was "service". Yes, we think of our saint-friend and list the many acts of service offered to the poor, disabled, the homeless, the abandoned, that merited her the title "Mother of Universal Charity".

Chris knows well those acts of service and has expressed that knowledge in her years of commitment to God's people with an indomitable spirit. Recently, however, she has suffered a disability that wreaks havoc on her freedom of availability. Macular degeneration! Now the one who was master of her time and activities depends on others to reach out in some of the services of love she was involved in.

Chris shared deeply about choosing service—how she might respond to this charism in 2011 even after twenty years as an Associate. She spoke of her new disability, with her loss of sight. Chris joined the book club in her new residence. There she realized that many elderly were having visual difficulties. The Holy Spirit spoke to her helping her to see in her own sight diminishment the opportunity to provide a service to those in the group, to reach out to their need. In typical Chris fashion she sought opportunities for these readers from the Olmstead Foundation in Buffalo and even extended her search to Albany to find ways to accommodate the readers' needs. And, this act of service emanating from her own disability became a gift for this group, members of a reading club.

Chris also offers a challenge to each of us who experience physical diminishment and the call of Jesus to take up our cross, to lift it in behalf of others, to offer our pain in behalf of others.

"Abba, Father, all things are possible to you. Take this cup away from me, but not what I will but what you will." With these words Jesus accepted the pain of suffering that would follow. He took up his cross as freely as he had accepted becoming man.

Onlookers challenged him "save yourself by coming down from the cross."

But this was Jesus' act of service . . . that he embraced what he was not in a role of diminishment—God, Creator, born in the likeness of man in all but sin. The God-man Jesus was born to suffer in our behalf. By that suffering Jesus saved us all from eternal suffering . . . that by his suffering, death and resurrection we might rise with him to eternal life.

And so Chris has seen the value of her diminishment as a call to be of true service in imitation of the One called to serve us.

"Take up your cross and follow me" remains the call to each of us as an opening to be of true service.

2668

Cell—Mania

I sat in my Campus Ministry office reminiscing about the day, conscious of Catholics joining many others among the Christian denominations to celebrate the Feast of the Annunciation, the message of Gabriel to Mary.

At one point during my day, still caught up in my thoughts, but a bit overtaken by a momentary gaze away from my computer, I was struck with the number of cell phone users who pass by my office door. They walk and talk, chatting away, connected mysteriously to some invisible friend or loved one, and (once again according to my observation) seem so oblivious to the world around them.

Cell phones, I thought: an incredible convenience for some, and an amazing invention, for sure. It's the kind of technology that offers us a reminder of the gifts that God provides through the blessing of human ingenuity.

I have one. I chose 2668 as the phone number as a way to keep me from mixing my office extension and my cell number, from forgetting which was which. A clever move, I thought. I kept it available and open to receive any emergency calls.

What about the cell phone users who had distracted me? It was not my imagination suggesting that theirs were not emergency conversations. I'd been privy to their idle chatter while in the elevators—otherwise dubbed (by me) public phone booths. Others had admitted chatting with a friend at the end of the hall (a distance of a city block away). Often their voices are raised in a public argument with an invisible target. All the while the students in their midst are also invisible and denied a "good morning" or a simple "hi" on the way.

Walking and talking. Immediacy over intimacy! No privacy, no live interaction even in a day when "reality" is in vogue on TV. Cell chatterers miss out on a chance to offer a cost free smile, or a kindly eye contact. It is missing those in our midst with an eye to eye rather than ear to ear visit.

The cell phone, as wonderful a convenience as it is, can disconnect us from our opportunity to share the most simple and valuable human experience—presence—to be with one another. What ever happened to passing by and leaving a "good morning" or a simple "hi" on the way?

Yes, I too use my cell phone. But it never replaces my being present to folks in my midst. I don't walk and talk. Should the phone ring when I am in "your" company, I ignore the call lest I lose what is important—the presence of "you" who has something to say to me—a message, a greeting . . . perhaps asking for my response.

The Annunciation—the day is set aside to honor the most awesome moment in human history, when centuries ago in a tiny village called "Nazareth", a very young and unmarried woman, indeed a mere teen, said "Yes" to the Angel Gabriel.

Scripture doesn't reveal where Mary was when the angel appeared to her. Was she in a corner of her home set aside for her as a bedroom? Or might she have been outside busy at a household chore? Perhaps she was sitting on a hill, resting and watching a sunset.

We might suspect that Mary was alone someplace rather than in the company of others since the angelic greeting was so intimate. There was no one to coax her, to remind her of the Jewish expectation of a Messiah, or to urge her to respond with caution because she was not married.

But what if . . . ? I couldn't help but think how different history would have been had Mary been busily chatting on a cell phone and oblivious to the presence of the Angel Gabriel, only to have missed the chance to say "Yes" to the Lord.

3705
The Spit Test

I gave my thumb a quick rub over my tongue and rubbed it across the signature on the letter I was investigating. It was a habit I acquired from who knows when or where. But it was effective in making my point. And just what was my point that day?

A Campus Minister invites a variety of people with as many concerns into the space called the Campus Ministry Centre. One young man who stepped into my confidence was Richard. He came with a background that was apparently disturbing his life and his ability to satisfy some spiritual yearning.

So many things came into play in his life as he continued the daily efforts of being a college student. He was gay but either wanted to change that identity or had been urged to pray it away. He had attended gatherings where the minister seemed to press the idea of a conversion. He had studied to be a minister via the internet but had no congregation to shepherd. At times he would conduct a simple service in the Campus Ministry setting. He was sincere but it was often an awkward ministerial attempt when the remains of the bread of the service were spread with peanut butter.

One day he was excited to show me the letter he had received from a minister who encouraged him to be "healed" of his gay identity by following the enclosed instructions. First, there was a swatch of cloth. He was advised to touch it for intercession as he prayed. So much for the argument of calling on the saints for intercession! Then there were the numbers included in the letter—3705. All he had to do was make a contribution, along with the prayer, for any combination—$3.70, $37.05, or $370.50, or perhaps $3, 705.

I was enraged by the letter and its false claims and its search for contributions. As though that cloth and dollars would free him from his being gay! It was thus that I snatched the letter and said "Let's do the spit test". As I expected, the spit failed to distort the apparent original signature on the letter. It was a form letter that deceived a yearning young man.

In the end, the young man studied Catholicism, was converted to the faith, and has been walking the journey of his life, committed to chastity and carrying his gay cross.

Spit! How and why did Jesus use spit to heal those who cried out for help? We hear of the blind man of Bethsaida who begged Jesus to touch him. Jesus led him outside the village. There he put "spittle" on the man's eyes and laid his hands on them. His sight was restored.

Are there some restoration properties of spit (spittle) that Jesus knew about? Was he perhaps offering a kind of baptism—a rising to new life? Twice he asked the man if he could see. Finally, scripture relates that "he could see everything distinctly". But Jesus didn't use this action in all his healings. Rather, he went about healing using very different actions—sometimes even without touching the one in need. All this falls into the mystery of the God-man and his ways.

Baptism relieves us of the darkness of life born in sin and leads us into the light of faith. It is out of this sacrament, this sign marked with water that we come to see distinctly and in amazement we sing: "I once was blind but now I see . . .".

Think of the ways we use spit to an advantage. We turn pages of a book or magazine, we separate bills as we count them, we lick the envelope to seal it, and we rub away a spot on a clean shirt . . .

We may even find ourselves in a place . . . away from a church or priest . . . marking a cross on the forehead three times as we perform an emergency baptism in the name of the Most Holy Trinity . . . perhaps using the only water available—spit.

8792

The End? Or, a Place to Pause?

I have been obsessively drawn to the TV program "Monk". Those who have spent seven years and repeats with this wannabe detective know his obsession with numbers, that everything counted must end up with an even number. Since this book must conclude someplace, and since it too is involved with numbers, I find it appropriate to end with an even number of my life tales or parables.

Appropriate? Only because of Monk, my Friday evening friend! There are more scoops on my life, more numbers to remind me of events. The question loomed for me. Should I continue or pause after the largest numbered episode—8791, the 63rd . . . both uneven numbers?

Perhaps this comment will serve to be the required even number of episodes in this book. The problem is what number will be used to place it properly as the last episode to be read. What would Monk do? How would he resolve this situation? How could this last episode become 8792? Perhaps in the rubble of Monk's numbers we find the solution:

8   The final season of the series-the 8th

7   Prominent characters included during the series: Monk, a Nurse, Cpt. Leland, Lt. Discher, Dr. Kroger (or Dr. Bell), an upstairs neighbor, and wife Trudy

9   The time Monk aired on my Friday viewings

2   Monk had 2 nurses—Sharona and Natalie (and two psychologists) during the series

Using these indicators, I feel justified in calling the last episode in this book"8792 The End . . . or, perhaps . . . just a pause!"

Jesus chose to call twelve. There is no scriptural offering of why he chose that number. One might see it as an even number. When the number was broken by Judas, the eleven chose someone to fill his place, to bring the chosen number back to twelve. An even number! It is interesting that the spiritual numbers in the bible are three and seven, both odd numbers. Oh! Three and seven are ten!

Yet, scripture does not suggest that the 12 be an end of the number of disciples. Rather, it records that many others were followers of Jesus and many others became believers as well. Jesus' commission: "go out and teach all nations . . . . !" Not an end . . . !

The **Woody Menu** Translated

The humor is in the Puns and Your "Order"

You order choices: **Select** numbers in order

1. Lover's Delight
2. Royal's Rival
3. Bug's choice
4. Neptune's Helper
5. Molar Digger
6. Royce's Partner
7. Dracula's Delight
8. Sleeping Relative
9. Bad Actor with Irish Eyes
10. Newport's Life
11. Mr. S's" Drippings
12. Stringy Skinny Helper
13. Mt. McKinley.
14. Wilkinson's Edge
15. Musical Fruit
16. Popeye's Amour
17. Pucker Power
18. Drunken Delmonte

You are **served** in the order selected—one item at a time

Spoon . . . Jello . . . Carrots . . . Fork . . . Tooth Pick . . .
Rolls . . . Tomato Juice . . . Napkin . . . Ham& Potatoes . . .
Water . . . Coffee . . . Celery . . . Baked Alaska . . . Knife . . .
Beans . . . Olives . . . Pickles . . . Fruit Cup

Enjoy!